# TOM CHATTO, APPRENTICE

To Tom Chatto, a lad of nearly seventeen fresh from the west of Ireland, Liverpool seems a magical city. Queen Victoria is on the throne, her Empire is growing. Liverpool is the second most important seaport in Britain—and Tom is sailing from there on his first voyage as an apprentice in sail. An adventurous life awaits him at sea, but with seven years' experience necessary before he can sit for his Master's Certificate, he has to learn the hard way.

# TOM CHATTO, APPRENTICE

# TOM CHATTO, APPRENTICE

*by*
Philip McCutchan

**Magna Large Print Books**
Long Preston, North Yorkshire,
England.

British Library Cataloguing in Publication Data.

---

McCutchan, Philip
   Tom Chatto, apprentice.

A catalogue record for this book is
available from the British Library

ISBN 0-7505-0754-3

First published in Great Britain by The Orion Publishing
Group, 1994

Published in Large Print February 1995 by arrangement with
The Orion Publishing Group & the copyright holder.

Magna Large Print is an imprint of
Library Magna Books Ltd.
Printed and bound in Great Britain by
T.J. Press (Padstow) Ltd., Cornwall, PL28 8RW.

# CHAPTER 1

Mr Patience's voice cut like a knife through the murk of Merseyside, roaring for'ard from the poop to travel angrily along the damp deck and among the bleary-eyed men struggling through the previous night's liquor fumes to identify the mass of ropes, the guys and the downhauls, the standing and the running rigging.

'O'Connor! See to that man, and quickly.'

Ahead of Tom Chatto, the bosun waved a hand in acknowledgement. 'Aye, sir,' he called back. Turning, he moved along the deck, rain-slippery and not yet cleaned of shoreside grease and muck, and seized hold, cruelly, of the man who had just brought up his stomach to add the stench of beer-sick and rum-sick to the sea smells of tarred rope and canvas. Upending the man, O'Connor pushed the screaming face into the trails of vomit, rubbing it up and down the deck planking. The man vomited again, then began a horrible dry retch. When he staggered to his feet there was murder in his eyes, but the bosun never gave him a chance before landing a heavy blow that put the seaman down like a log. Away to starboard, across the far side of the basin, a steam tug was seen approaching, and another bellow came from Mr Patience on the poop to apprise the hands of this fact.

Looking at the unconscious man lying in the vomit, Tom Chatto felt sick himself, sick to the very guts, but this was scarcely the time to show it. They were outward bound and he would get short shrift from everyone aboard, from Captain Landon downwards. Nevertheless, as the steam tug moved across towards the ship beneath the dull grey overcast of the Mersey River, he couldn't help feeling that all this was very different from the sober dignity of the Line's offices in Water Street—that the reality of being aboard a windjammer was very different from the rosy mental image.

Yesterday came back to Tom Chatto.

To a lad of nearly seventeen fresh from the West of Ireland, Liverpool had seemed a magic city. It was a sailor's town, was

Liverpool; none quite like it anywhere else on God's earth, Tom had been told. Solid and prosperous, like good Queen Victoria herself. The buildings, both civic and commercial, were tall and imposing and to Tom Chatto none were more imposing, nor more romantically worn with the soot and damp of Merseyside, than the one that was the home of the Porter Holt Shipping Company.

Goree House dominated Water Street with its columns and its tall windows, with the house-flag of the Porter Holt Line rain-soaked on its high staff, with the big polished brass plate that glowed warmly even through the morning's grey Mersey drizzle that dampened the pavements and sent the shipping clerks and the messengers of the Bank of Liverpool and the insurance companies' employees scurrying for the dryness and comparative warmth of their offices and their chest-high desks. And then there was the smell of Liverpool. Tom had smelled that smell only the once before, on the day he'd come with his father to be interviewed by the Board of Directors at the Porter Holt offices; but even so it had been unmistakable to him when, early this very morning, he had caught it again as the packet from Dublin had brought him once more into the Mersey: a smell made up from a magic mixture of mist and salt water and soot and tar laced with the fragrance of spices from the Orient; and laced again with the smoke from the steamers, dirty monsters that were gradually driving sail from all the world's seas.

Tom told the cabby to wait with his sea-chest and then went up the flight of broad stone steps, past that great brass plate inscribed with the name of the Line, between the tall, fluted columns, into a quiet and stately hall with an ornate ceiling and a beautifully curved staircase. Buckingham Palace, surely, could be no grander! Tom felt uncomfortable, out-of-place in his suit of thick, dark-blue pilot-cloth, his brand new badge-cap twisting in his hands. He turned sharply as he heard a sound behind him; he saw an elderly man coming up the steps, slowly, puffing a little, keeping his tall silk hat firmly and squarely on his head as he advanced into the hall with an air of assured importance. As he did so another man, dressed in black, with a high starched collar and sober cravat, came out from a doorway.

'Morning, Curtis,' the tall-hatted gentleman said briskly, rubbing his hands together as if to warm them.

'Good morning, Captain Bellamy, sir.' Curtis inclined his head, linking his hands in front of his frock coat. 'Mr John will be in presently...if you'd not mind waiting, sir?'

'Waiting—ha! I trust Mr John understands I haven't got all morning, Curtis. I have a ship to take out on the tide, y'know.'

'Quite so, sir.' Curtis coughed discreetly and shepherded the captain to a room across the hall the door of which bore the legend MASTERS' ROOM, and then, seemingly for the first time, became aware of Tom Chatto. 'Now, young fellow,' he said. 'What can I do for you?'

Tom said awkwardly, 'My name's Chatto —apprentice, joining the barque *Pass of Drumochter*,' and then, to be on the safe side, added politely, 'sir.'

'Ah, yes,' Curtis said, and nodded. 'Take a seat, young man. Mr Ralph will be in presently.'

Tom looked around, saw a row of chairs in a dark corner of the hall. He went across and sat, wondering as he did so how many years, how many miles of deep water, would pass before he would be admitted to the grandeur and dignity of the tall hat and the Masters' Room, how long before someone like Curtis would bob his head and address him by the magic word 'Captain'. He thought fleetingly of home, of the small town of Moyna in County Galway, of his father walking in his leisurely, pre-occupied way from the deanery to the chapter meeting that Tom knew would be taking place that morning; had it not been for this meeting, an important one in the diocese of Moyna, his father would have accompanied him—at least as far as the offices—on this momentous day of joining his first ship. Had his mother been alive...but better not to think about that. Tom fought down a sudden pang of homesickness and concentrated almost fiercely on thoughts of Mr Ralph, whom he was to see for his formal welcome into the Line's sea-going employment, and of Mr John who was the remote, austere and much respected Chairman of the Board. Mr John Porter, Mr Ralph Porter, Mr Henry Porter, all brothers, and Mr Edward and Mr Augustus Holt: Porter Holt was still an exclusively family business and it was firm in its belief in a strict paternalism; and one of the many duties of a father was to give all his household a welcome to the fold.

This welcome had been explained, or at any rate outlined, to Tom by Uncle Benjamin—strictly not an uncle but an old friend of his father—Captain Benjamin Brand, Master Mariner retired, Younger Brother of Trinity House, who had in fact recommended Tom to the Line.

'Mr Ralph personally sees all new apprentices in the Board Room before they report aboard their ships,' Uncle Benjamin had said, so long ago it seemed now. 'He'll talk to you about duty and responsibility. He lays it on a little thick, I'm told...but he's right, boy, he's right. Remember that.'

Tom did; he remembered it now, while he waited with more than a touch of nerves, watching the comings and goings of the clerks and messengers as the morning became busier. He had been waiting for a quarter of an hour, during which time Captain Bellamy had emerged twice from the Masters' Room with a gold watch held meaningfully in his hand, when Mr John and Mr Ralph, remembered from Tom's

13

previous visit, came in together. Mr John was the thin one, with a sharp but kindly face; Mr Ralph was portly, with a plump face and a pompous way of holding his head so that, even though he was short, he appeared constantly to be looking down his nose. Five minutes after the two directors had disappeared from the hall, and four minutes after Captain Bellamy had been admitted to Mr John's room, Tom was ushered into the presence by Curtis.

Mr Ralph was seated, not at the long, highly polished mahogany table used by the Board in session, but in one of two club-like leather armchairs beside a glowing fire.

'Good morning, Chatto. Come here, boy.'

'Yes, sir.' Tom felt his voice go nervously high, and cleared his throat to cover it. He advanced towards the end of the long room, beneath the many portraits on the walls; paintings in oil of past chairmen, from Sir Ebenezer, the brothers' father, back to one Joshua Porter, Esquire. They formed a study in the changing fashions of dress and hairiness, from wigs to side-whiskers or beards, from colourful brocaded coats to sober, honest coats of the black frock variety, and much gleaming white linen.

On the other side were the ships, past and present. *Annandale, Foyledale, Wensleydale, Wharfedale, Teesdale* and so on. There was history in this room and, with the expansion of the British Empire going on all the time, history was still in the making.

Tom came awkwardly to a halt in front of Mr Ralph.

The director stroked at his pudgy cheeks. 'Not like *that*, boy. Not like that.' He gestured. 'Your cap.'

'I—I beg your pardon, sir?'

'Your cap. Not in the hand...dangling like a farm labourer. Beneath the arm.' He clicked his tongue. 'Come here.'

'Yes, sir.' Tom moved quickly, fetching up by the arm of the leather chair. Mr Ralph reached out, grunting a little with the effort, took the cap and thrust it sideways beneath Tom's left arm, sandwiched between body and elbow, with the badge and the shiny peak facing forward. 'That's the way. Now. I'd advise you to carry it like that when you report to Captain Landon. Now. Sit down, Chatto, sit down.'

'Thank you, sir.' Tom backed. He went down with a sudden jerk as the chair's edge met the backs of his legs. He reddened, feeling he had made a fool of himself already, even before he'd entered the mystic world of an actual ship.

Abruptly Mr Ralph asked, 'How's your father, boy?'

'Well, sir, thank you.'

Mr Ralph nodded; the formal pleasantries were concluded. Mr Ralph, staring intently at Tom, said solemnly, 'Jodure-com.'

Tom stared.

'Ever heard that before?'

'No, sir—'

'Then learn it now, and remember it throughout your life. *Jo-du-re-com.* Job, duty, responsibility, command. In that order. With the emphasis on duty throughout. Let me tell you of one thing you must learn very quickly, boy.' Mr Ralph leaned forward, gazing solemnly into Tom's eyes; the red coals of the fire, and the flickering flames, threw curious shadows over his own face. 'It is this. You must be attentive and obedient to every order of your captain. His wish is your command. Aboard any vessel at sea, from the lowest fishing-smack to the enormous coal-burning steamships of the Cunard Line, the Master is the supreme

16

authority, over-riding the Line, the Board and the Chairman. That is expressed in official terms by the Board of Trade in London. For the duration of the ship's articles, that is to say from the moment the ship leaves the Mersey until her return from wherever she might have gone, the vessel is legally and in all respects delivered to the Master under God and ceases to be the Line's property. The articles themselves, which you will sign before departure, are an agreement between the Master and the crew—not between the Board and the crew. The Master is legally liable for all expenditure and disbursements, including payments to the crew. I repeat: the Master is supreme, he is all. Were even Mr John himself aboard he could not legally give orders to the Master at sea. And that is the position to which you aspire, boy, if you prove yourself worthy.' He coughed, withdrawing himself back into the deep armchair, and a gleam of humour came into his eyes. 'Naturally, we have every confidence that our appointed captains will not refuse to deliver up the ship to us at the end of the voyage.' This was a joke and Tom smiled politely.

What came next was not a joke. 'You will

be helping to carry a great responsibility across the seas, young man. The Board expects you to live up to our very high standards of efficiency and behaviour.' Mr Ralph brought out an enormous blue silk handkerchief and sneezed into it mightily. 'As to the day-to-day life on board, you are entering an exacting and dangerous profession and in many ways a rough one. Men who take ships to sea are not saints, young Chatto. A ship is like neither school nor a deanery in the West of Ireland. There is coarse talk, in the half-deck and in the saloon as often, perhaps, as in the fo'c'sle. When men go ashore they take strong drink—but take care that you are yourself sober. Be attentive to your duty, let me repeat again, and to the orders of all who are set in authority over you. Do this, and you should not fail in your chosen career. There are just two other things.' He paused, then leaned forward once again, his face more solemn than ever. 'Women,' he said. 'Be circumspect in your approach to the women of the ports overseas; they can do harm to an apprentice's career. They are best avoided altogether. But no doubt,' Mr Ralph added, 'your father has spoken to you of this.'

Tom said, 'No, sir.' He flushed; he could no more imagine the Dean of Moyna speaking of such matters than he could imagine him pocketing the collection at matins.

'No?' Mr Ralph raised his eyebrows. 'I see. That being the case, I shall act *in loco parentis.*' He pursed his lips, hummed and ha'ed until Tom believed he was about to hear all the basic facts of life, naked and unadorned as he'd heard them at school. But such was not to be the case. All Mr Ralph did was to wag a finger and say pontifically, 'Women, my boy, are best kept at arm's length until you have many more years behind you. Make no mistake—I know well what a young man's instincts are, and these are natural. They must, however, be held in check. A man is a man and not an animal. The women of the ports are prowling beasts of prey. Do you understand me, boy?'

'Yes, sir.'

'Good. Now we come to the last thing, which is perhaps the most important of all. *Be loyal.* Yes, above all, young Chatto, be loyal. You will grow to manhood in the hardest of all worlds, the world of the deep-water windjammer. Loyalty is the attribute that tempers the hardships and makes them bearable in the darkest hours.'

Mr Ralph rose to his feet, heaving a vast stomach from the armchair. 'That is all, Chatto. Welcome to our company. Do well. Work hard. Do not be swift to count the hours when your duty bears hardly upon you. Smile in adversity, be willing, be cheerful. Good-day to you, young man. See Curtis. He will call you a cab to take you to your ship.'

Tom said, 'I have a cab waiting, sir, thank you.'

'Ah.' Mr Ralph raised his eyebrows again. 'Extravagance is *not* a virtue,' he said.

It was only when he was outside the room that Tom realized he'd said scarcely a word himself. Jodurecom, Tom thought, and shook his head in wonderment. It sounded like some kind of patent cure-all. Which, within its particular context, it perhaps was when he came to think of it...

And so from staid and solemn dignity to the harsh tones of Mr Patience, First Mate.

The cab took Tom Chatto out of Water Street, past the Bank of Liverpool and down towards the great sprawl of Liverpool docks.

Some 1,614 acres together with Birkenhead, 36 miles of quay...after the Port of London, Liverpool was the chief seaport of Great Britain, and the tonnage owned there not only exceeded the tonnage of the entire German Empire but was also three times the tonnage owned by all the United States of America. Tom Chatto felt a thrill of pride in the knowledge that he was now a part of all this challenging commerce, one of the cogs, however unimportant so far, who would keep the wheels of Empire grinding on. Britain, as well he knew, depended wholly for her very survival upon her seaborne trade, and thus upon her ships and the shell-backs who sailed them through the storms of wind and water. These were the sinews of her being, of her current expansion into the greatest Empire the world had ever known. From Liverpool and ports like it her regiments were kept supplied and in good heart to fight the battles of the Queen-Empress who from Windsor Castle ruled a quarter of the world's inhabitants. The ships of

England were the life-line that kept an empire and a way of life together and it was an exciting and important task that lay ahead for Tom Chatto, emerging from the semi-rural quietness of a deanery of the Protestant Church of Ireland...

Behind the cab-horse, behind the gusts of breath steaming from its nostrils, Tom looked out at the grey day and the stone temples of money and trade and power. He heard the clang and rattle of the great Liverpool tramway, commenced a quarter of a century earlier as the first one of importance in all Britain. He saw the smart carriages of the prosperous merchants, the men who were growing with the Empire. There were more tall hats and frock coats, and silver-headed canes, and lavender-coloured gloves. There were also the others: the poor, the men who went along with heads bent against the drizzle, shoulders hunched into thin garments, men wearing cloth caps and mufflers if they were lucky, the women in bonnets and shawls, the children largely barefoot, all representing the other side of the coin of Empire.

Soon Tom had entered the docks and the cab was trundling along behind the cargo sheds and warehouses that were filled with incoming and outgoing cargoes, with wool and grain from Australia, raw cotton, beef, mutton, bacon and hams; with manufactured goods going the other way—iron and steel, wool and cotton garments, mill work, machinery—waiting to be put into the slings aboard the outward-bounders at the berths. Tom noted that there were plenty of steamers in the basins: but even so, the port was still a place of timber and cordage, still a forest of masts and yards raking into the sky above the busy, littered decks. Everywhere there was the sight and sound of movement—the derricks of the steamers lifting the slings with the steam-winches rattling and belching, ships' mates calling orders, stevedores shouting to one another as they heaved at the cased goods with their shining cargo hooks.

The cab came round the angle of one of the sheds and approached the waterside. Tom saw the name on the bow of a sturdy three-masted barque: *Pass of Drumochter.* He saw the Porter Holt house-flag drooping from the main truck, and the Red Ensign at the staff aft on the poop. He felt a sense of awe as he pushed open the cab door and got out into the drizzle, into the distinctive smell of a ship: pitch, and tarred rope, and canvas.

Tom felt suddenly as uncomfortable as he had felt in the offices of the Line. He had arrived; and now he was committed. And everything was very, very strange.


# CHAPTER 2

'Stand from under, there, you bloody little fool!'

Tom jumped, looked up, and dodged fast as he saw a heavy crate swing in, netted on a whip leading from the derrick-head. A few inches more and that would have taken his head from his shoulders, a fact that the owner of the voice, a big man, dark, in his late thirties and wearing a badge-cap, was not slow to point out. Tom's cabby had brought his sea-chest aboard and had dumped it on the deck a few yards from the fore hatch from which the covers had been removed. As the sling was sent down into the hold the dark man, a person of obvious authority, suspended operations and, scrambling nimbly around the hatch coaming and the litter of gear lying on deck, strode across towards Tom.

'You're anxious to commit suicide, boy, is that it?'

'Why no, sir, I—I—'

'Whom, may I enquire, have I the honour of addressing?'

'My name's Chatto, sir, joining—'

'I thought as much. Never been to sea before, have you?'

'No, sir, I've—'

'You've answered the question, boy, so now you'll hold your tongue and speak again only when spoken to. You'll learn. The first thing you'll learn, here and now, is to keep an eye lifting aloft, that's if you want to live. As for me, apart from the mess made by a squashed body and the paper-work that follows, I don't much care if you live or not, but I dare say you've a mother who does. The next thing you'll learn is equally important if you want to go on living, and that is, I'm Mr Patience, First Mate. My name belies me as you'll discover. When I say jump—*you jump!* When I say I want a thing done, I mean five minutes ago, not next Monday. And after that, there's something else you'll learn never to do again.'

'What's that, sir?' Tom met Mr Patience's eye.

'What you're doing now, youngster. Which is to hold up the loading of a barque due to clear for foreign by tomorrow morning. That's what. Poor start, boy. Never, never hang around on deck. Either lend a hand, or get the hell out. Is that clear?'

'Yes, sir.' Tom's face was crimson; all this had taken place loudly before a grinning crowd of stevedores and seamen. It had been unfair, but Mr Ralph had spoken of a cheerful willingness. 'I'm sorry, sir.'

Mr Patience nodded, folded his arms across a deep chest, and seemed to be waiting for something. Tom was puzzled; he wished to be polite and helpful but had no idea what the First Mate might be expecting of him. After a moment Mr Patience snapped, 'Well, boy?'

Tom stared, shifted his feet and wished for the deck to swallow him. Mr Patience roared, 'Obey the order, boy, obey the order!'

'Which order, sir?' Even his ears were burning now.

'Which order he says!' The Mate's eyes rolled heavenwards. 'God roast you, boy, did I not order you either to lend a hand or get the hell out?'

'Yes, sir—'

'And you can't lend a hand because you don't bloody well know how to—do you?'

'Not yet, sir, but I'll—'

*'Then get the hell out!'*

Tom turned and ran, not knowing where he was going, though in fact it was aft, where less work was in progress and which was the safer way since it didn't lead past Mr Patience. But he was brought up all standing by another bellow from his tormentor.

'Take that damned chest with you, boy.'

Tom turned and ran back and, seizing one of the rope grommets secured to the chest, began dragging it away. Mr Patience seemed to be verging on a fit. 'I beseech and implore you, *Mister* Chatto, to consider my decks. Dirty I know they are, and covered with traces of the shore, and trampled by stinking, lubberly stevedores—but they are not yet scratched and scored.' The First Mate filled his lungs. *'Don't drag it, carry it!'*

Tom was close to tears by this time, but held them back by a supreme effort. To blub would be something he'd never live down. He bent and heaved at the rope handle of the sea-chest; he stumbled, and slipped on the greasy deck. There was a shout of laughter from around the fore hatch. Mr Patience danced with anger, real or assumed for the benefit of his audience. 'God give us both strength, *Mister* Chatto—me, to put up with you throughout what's going to be the longest voyage of my life, and you, to lift that damned chest! Make an effort, boy, make an effort.'

Straining every muscle, Tom got the heavy chest onto his back. The cabby, long in the back for carrying, and short in the legs, true peasant build, had managed with practised ease; Tom was far from practised. Somehow he steadied himself and wobbled off along the deck, moving dead slow, feeling for all the world like a tortoise. From behind came a ragged, ironic cheer and then in the next breath the sound of Mr Patience urging the men back to work. Tom had staggered as far aft as a square deckhouse set amidships when another voice said, 'That's as far as you need go, kid. Put down the chest. Take it easy—let it slide down—wait, I'll give you a hand.'

Tom saw blue-clad legs thrust into leather seaboots. Thankfully he felt his burden ease away. He stood upright. A young man was grinning at him, a youth some three or four years older than himself, tall and well built and with thick brown hair under his cap. He had a pleasant face and manner. Tom said, 'Thank you, sir.'

The young man nodded. 'It's not a bad principle,' he said, 'to call anything that moves aboard a ship, sir. When you're as green as you are, that is. But in fact I'm one you *don't* call sir. I expect you're Chatto?'

'Yes—'

'We've been expecting you. I'm Jim Wales, senior apprentice.' He gestured towards the deckhouse behind him, a wooden structure barely six feet in height with a handrail running around it, a handrail Tom was to be thankful for often enough in the heavy weather that was to signpost so many of the days ahead. 'Half-deck,' Wales said. 'Where you live. And the rest of us apprentices. Come on in—bring the chest and be careful how you handle it inside.'

He turned and led the way along a narrow alley that ran between the half-deck house itself and another structure which, he said, was where the petty officers—carpenter, bosun, sailmaker, cook —lived, with the galley just for'ard of it again. Then he ushered Tom into a dark space about twelve feet long by eight wide, a space almost entirely filled with eight bunks set in tiers, four on either side, with one tiny porthole giving dim light from aft. Wales gave Tom a hand to slide his sea-chest under one of the lower bunks.

'Eight berths as you see,' he said, 'but only four apprentices.'

'How's that?'

Wales straightened so far as the deckhead would permit. 'Porter Holt take on only the number of lads they know they'll be able to offer officers' berths to later. They're good employers.' He added, 'Many of the lines take on excess apprentices as cheap labour. But not Porter Holt.'

Tom nodded. 'There's one other new apprentice joining, isn't there?'

Wales laughed. 'He's already turned up, but he didn't stay long. He left his chest yesterday and then Mama took him off for a slap-up lunch and a night in the Adelphi Hotel in Lime Street. He'll be back...and I'll say this for you: you had the sense not to bring your mother.'

Tom said in a flat voice, 'She's dead.'

'Oh—I'm awfully sorry, old lad.' Jim Wales was embarrassed. 'I'd never have said—'

'It's all right.'

Wales seemed to be searching for something to say. He found it. 'Did I gather from the shouting that you'd met our First Mate?'

Tom said he had.

'Well,' Wales said kindly, 'don't let him worry you too much. He's not so bad when you get used to him. At least he's fair. Treats everyone like a village idiot—except the Old Man of course.' He added, 'And the Old Man's wife, but that's a different story. Did you know she was aboard, by the way?'

Again Tom nodded. Uncle Benjamin had told him and his father about Captain Theodore Landon whom he had known, not personally, but by reputation. Captain Landon had owned the *Pass of Drumochter* until a couple or so years ago, and his wife had sailed with him on every voyage since their marriage—except one, when she had given birth to a daughter, a daughter who had since died. Landon had been almost the last of the owner-masters and the advance of steam had taken away his cargoes and forced him to sell out to Porter Holt who, as a large company, could still make a profit in sail. Uncle Benjamin had gone on to say that Porter Holt, that considerate family firm, had made three concessions to the *Pass of Drumochter*'s former owner: because he was a first-rate Master Mariner with a fine record, he'd been retained in command; the name of his ship had not been altered to conform with the Porter Holt names; and his wife, who was many years his junior in age, had been allowed to continue sailing with him aboard what had been their home.

'When shall I meet the Captain?' Tom asked now.

His elbows resting on the upper bunk behind him, Jim Wales said, 'Patience'll take you along when the hands knock off. The Old Man's ashore at the moment on business.' Wales added, 'Like to look around the ship, young 'un?'

'Yes, I—'

'I'll go and ask Patience,' Wales said. He went off and was back in a couple of minutes. 'Permission granted,' he said. 'Ready?'

'Yes. And thank you very much.'

'It's a pleasure.'

Tom followed the senior apprentice out of the half-deck and was led aft towards the poop. Below the break of the poop Wales pointed out the entry through the alleyway to the saloon and the Master's and officers' quarters. On the poop itself was a hatch that also gave access to the Master's alleyway. Up here too was the wheel where, in bad weather, two helmsmen would be lashed for their own safety against the seas that could thunder up from aft to overwhelm them. Tom looked for'ard along the deck. Wales glanced at his intent face and, smiling, said, 'Yes, she's a fine sight from here right enough, but nothing to what she's like with all set to the royal t'gallants and a fair wind behind. Then she's magnificent, really magnificent. You'll see. She's no flyer like *Cutty Sark* or *Thermopylae*, but she's not slow either, and she handles grandly.'

'Have you been aboard her long?' Tom asked.

'Ever since Porter Holt took her over—just under three years. That's two voyages. By the time we pick up the channel pilot again, I'll be a few months overdue to sit for second mate.' There was quiet pride in his voice but he grinned and said self-deprecatingly. 'The Old Man says that's all to the good—I'll have a chance to learn a bit more in the extra time.'

'I don't suppose you need to, do you?'

Wales aimed a friendly blow at him. 'Don't flatter, it doesn't suit you. Of course I need to. At sea a man never stops learning. And it's experience that counts. In other words—time.'

'What'll you do when you've passed for second mate?'

Wales shrugged and looked up at the tall masts. 'Oh, I'll stay in sail till I've passed for master, of course, but after that...well, I don't know yet. Maybe I'll stay with the Line a year or two, get a berth as first mate. After that I'll have to go into steam. I'll be damn sorry to do it, but a man has to make a living and there's no real future left in sail. Not in the long run. I hear even Porter Holt are likely to build steamers soon. If they do, I'll stay with them if they'll have me.'

They moved aft. Wales continued with his theme. 'Take Mr Patience. Thirty-six and still First Mate. That's no good to a man. He's been a first mate ten years and still waiting for dead men's shoes.'

'Why doesn't he go into steam, then?'

Wales gave a shout of laughter. 'Patience, in steam? He'd as soon go down a coal mine. He's a first-class sail man and he knows it. Steam—why, it'd be like driving a tram.' He looked upwards, and Tom followed his gaze, up the masts to the trucks so far above, along the great yards with which the masts were crossed with the footropes hanging in curves below them, along the sails themselves now furled along the yards, waiting to be shaken out when, next day, the barque would be towed out of the Mersey River to pick up a wind and head south down the Irish Sea for the Bishop Rock. 'How high are the masts?' Tom asked in something like awe.

'The main truck's a hundred and forty feet from the deck, the fore and mizzen a little less. That's a devil of a long way to fall. And it's hard enough to keep on the footropes sometimes, say off the pitch of the Horn, with the old girl rolling her rails under and the ropes and sails stiff with ice...and a full gale doing its level best to snatch you off. All the pulley-hauley work's done manually, by the way—we've no donkey boiler to haul the braces over, and bracing the yards isn't funny with the decks awash up to a man's shoulders. Specially when half the hands you get these days don't know the difference between a clew-garnet and the galley funnel till they've been licked into shape. I include you in that, young Chatto. Know what a clew-garnet is?'

'No,' Tom answered, 'but at least I can recognize the galley funnel—I think!'

Wales laughed and clapped him on the shoulder. 'That's half way to being a seaman, then.' He gave Tom a critical, sweeping look. 'Not much muscle yet...but at least there's no fat. You'll toughen up fast enough—you'll be surprised.'

Tom hoped he would. Wales was well-set-up, with powerful arms and thighs and plenty of depth of chest and breadth of shoulder. A young bull, full of health and vitality, with a happy, contented face and honest, clear eyes. Command material, Tom thought with envy, far from sure that the same would be said of him when he was approaching the end of his four years' sea time necessary before he could sit the examination for his second mate's certificate of competency. It was a long business: with second mate behind him there would be two more years for first mate, another year again for master—and after that would begin the long wait for dead men's shoes...

Wales led him for'ard, back past the half-deck, past the fore hatch where Mr Patience was still working cargo. The actual loading, Wales said, was a stevedore's job; but the First Mate was responsible for the proper stowage of the cargo so that the vessel would be at her proper marks for all the seas through which she would pass on her long voyage. Different oceans had different water densities, and so the marks were different. Seventeen years before, in 1876, Samuel Plimsoll had established his famous Plimsoll Line; Mr Patience was bound by this. And not this alone; his was the often arduous and intricate task of working out on paper the positioning of the different varieties in a mixed cargo so that they were properly stowed with regard to fore-and-aft trim, with dangerous cargoes separately stowed in conformity with precise regulations, and seeing that shifting-boards and battens were correctly sited. Also that cargoes for en route ports were stowed in such a manner that the destination-port cargoes didn't have to be unloaded along the way.

Wales explained all this. 'Patience isn't the right name,' he said lightly, 'when the jigsaw doesn't work out. I've seen him tear his hair out by the roots before now, and the Old Man's missus has gone white from the swear words. Then, of course, there's the bulk grain cargoes. Rice, for instance. You get that on the Far East run. Since we're Australia bound, we're spared that this time.'

'Is rice difficult, then?'

'It can be. Rice swells when it gets wet. If a sea starts a hatch cover, say, and gets into the hold...well, the rice can sink you. Split the ship—literally. It's been known before now. We were talking of dead men's shoes...there's plenty of ways you can die aboard a windjammer! Or at least be maimed for life. No joke to be flattened by a falling yard or carried overboard by a torn sail, that sort of thing. Come on and I'll show you the fo'c'sle-head and the anchors and windlass, then the tween-decks and the trunkways to the holds.'

The drizzle kept up all through the day. At noon the hands went to dinner and were back at work an hour later; at one bell in the first dog watch the last of the cargo came inboard and when all was shipshape below the hatch covers went on, the planks being slotted into place, the canvas tarpaulins hauled across and wedged down hard by the carpenter's hammer. This done, Mr Patience set the ship's crew to clean down. Buckets of water were produced despite the drizzle and the hands went to work with brooms and squeegees. When the ship was cleaned to his satisfaction Mr Patience passed the word that the men could go ashore, and, in a body, with anticipatory looks on their faces, they went. Tom Chatto was told, along with the other newly-joined apprentice, one Horatio Mainprice who had now been re-delivered by his mother, to wash and tidy himself before being taken to the saloon for introduction to the Master.

Tom considered Horatio Mainprice to be a fine nautical-sounding name, but any bearing of name on character was given the lie by its owner's appearance, which was somewhat sly with a tendency to be supercilious in addition.

The two apprentices followed Mr Patience along the officers' cabin alleyway to the saloon, where Captain Theodore Landon was sitting in front of a coal-fired grate that looked to Tom an extremely dangerous comfort to be taking to sea in a wooden-walled ship. As the youngsters entered, a fair-haired woman of around thirty years, who had been sewing, rose to her feet smiled at them, wished them good evening and went out by the after door. She was decidedly pretty and had a fine figure. Mr Patience was looking at her and Tom fancied there was a constraint in the air, but hadn't time to think about this, for the patriarchal figure of Captain Landon was getting courteously up.

The Captain reached out a hand. He was an impressive man; like a prophet of old he had a mass of white hair that came down his cheeks to join a white beard. Tall and broad, he could have been frightening and, no doubt, Tom decided, often was; but the blue eyes, though grave and somehow withdrawn, looked friendly at this moment of first meeting.

In an abrupt, rather shy voice, Landon said, 'Welcome aboard my ship, young fellows. I'm delighted to have you, delighted.' He paused. 'This state of affairs will persist for so long as you are attentive to your duties, willing to learn, and obedient to the orders of your superiors. I trust I shall have no cause for complaint. To the end that you learn your job as seamen so that you may become officers of a fine service, I shall always be available for advice and guidance—though not for you to come running with grievances against your superiors, who are fair men, as I trust I am myself. Now. Have you anything you wish to ask, either of you?'

Tom said, 'No, thank you, sir.'

Captain Landon raised bushy eyebrows. 'Oho! So here we have the young man who knows it all already, have we?' His voice had lost is abruptness; it was rumbling now with a kind of restrained amusement and the eyes were twinkling in the light from an oil-lamp hanging in gimbals above the big saloon table. He repeated, 'Have we?'

'Oh, no, sir, no indeed,' Tom said earnestly. 'I know nothing yet. It was just that...there is so much to learn that I couldn't think of where to begin, sir.'

Landon laughed out loud at that. 'Well said, boy, well said! Bovine stupidity depresses me, but not honest ignorance. Now you, Mainprice. Well?'

Horatio Mainprice cleared his throat, watched Captain Landon with a sharp and beady eye, but looked away before he spoke. He said, 'I wish to ask about laundry facilities on board, sir...and whether or not these are free.'

Landon's face didn't move a muscle. He didn't answer the question but spoke to the First Mate. 'Mr Patience, which in your opinion is the worst—stupidity that appears in Mainprice's case to be not stupidity in fact but only an improperly ordered mind, or a laudable but fussy cleanliness laced with avarice?'

Mr Patience ran a hand over his jaw and pondered. Then he said, 'The Lord knows, sir, I'm sure I do not. But I'll be finding out once we're behind the tug and after...oh, I'll be finding out right enough, all the way to Sydney Heads!'

Captain Landon smiled and said, 'I have my answer, gentlemen. I'm well content to leave the rest in the hands of Mr Patience. That is all. You may go. Thank you, Mr Patience.'

As they moved for'ard along the open deck Mr Patience seemed in something of a temper. He said, 'Laundry my backside. You'll do your own in a bucket—and be thankful for the cold water to do it in. Oh, you'll learn, the pair of you.' He brought out a turnip-shaped watch, looked at it, and announced, 'Tea, or if you prefer the word, supper, will be ready in the galley. Newest joined gets the job of fetching it to the half-deck. Your mates'll tan the hide off you if you don't smack it about.'

Patience left them then, going about some business of his own. Mainprice muttered something about the fellow being an uneducated boor. The youth seemed very disconsolate; Tom wondered how he had ever got past Mr John and Mr Ralph; and came to the conclusion that there had been influence somewhere along the line, a conclusion that later turned out to be accurate.

# CHAPTER 3

Supper, or tea, consisted of what Jim Wales called cracker hash, a mixture of salt beef and broken biscuits, quite appetizing no doubt after weeks at sea, but scarcely so now, when Tom's palate was fresh from Irish pastures and the well-provided deanery table. The Very Reverend Desmond Chatto was inclined to do himself well and did not stint his family and servants of the good things in food and, to some extent, drink. It had not been unknown for Tom to share in a bottle of a light table wine since his sixteenth birthday. The *Pass of Drumochter*'s half-deck was accorded no such luxuries, though tonight the cracker hash was accompanied by fresh vegetables.

'You'll not be getting *them* much longer,' Wales said, eating with relish, 'so make the most of 'em now. Don't waste the hash either...you'll be begging for it once we're at sea.'

'What is it?' Mainprice asked disparagingly, pushing half the mess to the side of his plate in defiance of Wales' advice.

Wales told him. 'Salt junk and hard tack. What happens is this: you save some salt junk from your dinner, mix it up with hard tack, and take it to the galley to be baked by Slushy—that's the cook. Then you have something for your tea.' Wales looked critically at Mainprice. 'You eat all you can *when* you can, nipper. Build up against the times when you'll go hungry, with the fires drawn in bad weather.'

Mainprice scowled. 'I wish you wouldn't call me nipper,' he said complainingly.

Wales laughed. 'You're a month or two younger than Chatto. That, by seafaring tradition, makes you the nipper. You'll just have to get used to it, for this voyage at least.'

Horatio Mainprice scowled again but made no further protest. Then, looking up, he said, 'This business of vegetables at sea. Or rather, the lack of them. Don't you get scurvy from a lack of fresh vegetables?'

'Yes,' Wales said cheerfully.

'It doesn't sound very healthy.'

'It isn't. Not if it goes on too long. Usually, it doesn't. It's only when you get a run of bad luck...weather against you, so you're late in making port and picking up fresh provisions. Anyway, for God's sake, don't start worrying now. The Old Man's got a reasonably well-stocked medicine chest and he's good at diagnosing apprentices, believe you me!' Musingly he added, 'He has a favourite remedy and it's good.'

'What is it?' Mainprice asked.

Wales met Tom's eye and winked. 'Jodurecom,' he said with a straight face. Tom stifled a laugh.

Mainprice wriggled irritably and said, 'You're pulling my leg.'

Wales grinned. 'Well, of course, you'll have had Mr Ralph's little homily—you too, Chatto?'

Tom nodded, glad to note that Jim Wales seemed to view Mr Ralph's *aide-memoire* in the same light as himself; a shared sense of humour made for a kind of bond. With a grin Wales went on, 'Very effective in all kinds of ways is Jodurecom. As a matter of fact, the Old Man's variety is better known as Black Draught. It tastes filthy, and the Old Man's missus administers it every Sunday forenoon to everyone aboard under the age of eighteen. That's Board of Trade regulations, let me add. Till the system gets used to it, you'll be glued to the heads for hours after taking it.'

'Heads?'

'Nautical name for the WC, my lad. Luckily for you, the ship's reasonably up-to-date and nicely fitted out. The inboard heads are for the use of the Master and officers and, by the kindly intervention of Mrs Landon, the apprentices as well. The rest of the crew use the old-fashioned methods...they dangle over the side, holding onto the gunwales—from the fore part of the ship, hence the traditional name, heads.' Wales pushed his empty plate away and yawned. In a friendly way he asked, 'Where d'you come from, by the way, nipper?'

'Why d'you want to know that?'

Wales gaped, flushing darkly. 'I don't—if you don't want to tell me.' He was utterly astonished at such a reaction. 'What's up with you?'

Mainprice didn't answer at first; then he said reluctantly, 'My home's in Southsea. That's the better part of Portsmouth. My father's in practice there, a GP.'

Wales gave a slow nod, as though some

light had broken through. 'Portsmouth, home of the RN,' he said quietly. 'Any connection, nipper?'

Mainprice didn't meet his eye. 'I wanted to enter the navy, if you call that a connection.'

'Then why didn't you?'

Sullenly Mainprice said, 'Oh, reasons.' Then he expanded, though it seemed to be with a conscious effort. 'My guv'nor wouldn't cough up to send me to the *Britannia.* Porter Holt's premium was—rather less. And I have an uncle who knows the Porter family...married a sister in fact. My uncle happens to be an admiral.'

'So Uncle helped? Or Auntie?'

'Yes.'

Wales said seriously, 'If I were you, nipper, I'd not make that too widely known aboard. And I'd forget the RN from now on. I've nothing against the Queen's ships, but the fact is, you're aboard a merchantman now. We have our traditions, too, and we're inclined to believe we're doing a more useful job than the warships in times of peace. Just remember that.' Abruptly, frowning now, he turned to Tom Chatto, 'What made *you* come to sea?' he asked.

Tom's answer was simple and direct: 'I always wanted to.' He left it at that, and so, after an appraising stare in the light of the oil-lamp, did Wales, who started a conversation with the fourth apprentice, a youth named Ted Allan who had completed one voyage with him. The two discussed the possibilities of the forthcoming run, which would be through the South Atlantic to Cape Horn for Valparaiso in Chile, thence south and west across the Pacific to Sydney in Australia. They yarned with all the knowledgeableness of seasoned men, showing off to some extent before the green newcomers. Ted Allan was small and fair, a very different sort from Wales—perky, like a sparrow. He was the son of a tenant farmer from near Fakenham in Norfolk, and from his occasional references to the land as he talked to Wales, Tom formed the impression that Norfolk was too small, too constricting, for him to want to spend his life on his father's or anyone else's farm. He seemed decent enough but didn't carry the weight of Jim Wales, who had the air of a born seaman; was, as Tom had thought earlier, marked already with the

49

indelible stamp of someone who would carry command as a woman wears a glove, unconscious of it. Yet he hadn't, Tom suspected, the background advantages of Horatio Mainprice or of himself. There was a roughness about his accent that spoke of humble origins and a lack of formal education though his speech itself gave evidence of an effort at self-improvement.

That night the apprentices turned in early and doused the lamp. They would, Wales said, be up bright and early next morning.

That first night aboard a sailing ship was in some ways a frightening one to Tom Chatto, since it held some of the emotion of the cast die. As he lay awake in his narrow top bunk, listening to the sleeping noises of his messmates and to the variegated night-sounds of the Port of Liverpool—occasional voices from the nightwatchmen on ship and shore, lurching footsteps along the deck outside as the drunks among the crew came back aboard with their money spent; the cries of seagulls, the distant sounds from the foghorns of ships moving out on the last of the night tide, the more distant sound of a railway train—Tom's doubts, and in fact there had been a few at the last minute as it were before leaving home, came flooding over him like a strong current. There was perhaps time yet to back out. If he was to go aft to Captain Landon and beg for his release from his indentures, the Captain would no doubt be pleased to be rid of him, glad that he'd shown his lack of courage in good time to be sent away ignominiously.

But of course he could never do that. In point of fact, such an act would call for even more courage than to stay and go to sea next morning with the *Pass of Drumochter*. Besides, in his heart he *wanted* to go to sea in her, for another reason than the one he'd given Jim Wales—which happened to be entirely true: he did want to go to sea, he did want to command a ship; but he wanted also to prove himself. This was not, in fact, a particularly original desire, but Tom Chatto was young enough not to be aware of this and it loomed large in his mind as he lay and stared at the deckhead above the bunk, a deckhead that was just visible in the light from the dockside lamps filtering through the porthole and which was no more than twelve inches from the tip of his nose and thus claustrophobic in the extreme. A fat apprentice, he thought foolishly, would have a thin time...he grinned briefly; that was the kind of joke his father liked to make; the family was well accustomed to such.

Thinking of his father brought the ache of homesickness.

It wasn't that he'd ever been very close to his father—he had not; the Dean of Moyna was too pre-occupied with his duties and his calling and his books, mainly ecclesiastical ones, to engage himself overmuch in the affairs of his offspring. But he was his father nevertheless, had loomed rather larger since the sudden death of Tom's mother in a boating accident on Lough Corrib three years before; and he represented home.

Tom thought nostalgically of the rambling deanery, of its well-loved garden enclosed by old, high walls, of his own bedroom, austere but with all his own possessions to give it warmth and comfort and personality, a room he might not see again for many thousands of miles and very many months. He thought of his childhood's pony, now in retirement; in his mind he rode again with his friends, largely the sons of the cathedral clergy, on long explorations of the wild and beautiful Connacht country where the land was free and open and windswept, lying in the lee of the purple hills, the hills of home that ran down to the broad Atlantic Ocean...to the shores of Connemara with their wild rollers when the wind blew off the sea, and the quiet, clear pools in the rocks at Roundstone when the wind dropped and the rain ceased and the sun broke through to shine with a clear brightness peculiar to that remote West of Ireland landscape dotted with thatched, whitewashed cottages and criss-crossed with dry-stone walls. He thought of the fish in the lough, of the great salmon leaping the weir lower down by Galway City in their due season; of the Galway Blazers meeting, sometimes in the deanery grounds though the Chattos themselves had never ridden to hounds; of the 88th Foot, Irish soldiers of the Queen, Connacht's own regiment of Rangers, whom Tom had often seen marching through the town behind the fifes and drums, their Colours borne along by the guard whose subaltern was Tom's own brother Philip, now serving in India.

Thinking of Philip, Tom thought again of his father.

The good dean had been much pleased with Philip, the elder son, when he'd decided upon the army. After all, though a poor enough financial prospect for an officer without private means, it was a gentleman's life. The dean had been equally pleased when the second son, Edward, had expressed a preference for the Church; and had then metaphorically sat back, albeit with little hope in the case of a younger son who liked the outdoor life, for Tom to complete the gentlemanly trilogy and enter the profession of the Law.

When the subject had been discussed and the hoped-for had not happened, the dean had looked startled but had said only, 'H'm.'

And then, when Tom had said, diffidently, that he wanted to go to sea but had no interest in the Queen's ships, the dean had suspected accurately that the source of young Tom's desires had been Uncle Benjamin. When Tom had been adamant the dean had conceded: he had other things on his mind and Tom after all was no more than a younger son. He had sent for his housekeeper, Mrs Murphy, and bade her send a telegraph message to Tom's mentor. Two weeks later Uncle

Benjamin had jolted up from Galway City on a sidecar, known to the English but not to the Irish as a jaunting car. It had been a long journey for an elderly gentleman and Uncle Benjamin had been thirsty; Mrs Murphy, knowing the Captain well enough, had seen to it that a small cask of whiskey was at hand in the dean's study when the old man had arrived.

Tom had been out in a sailing dinghy in Galway Bay when Uncle Benjamin had disembarked from the sidecar, but he had been told the Captain was coming and, of course, he knew why: Uncle Benjamin's brain was to be well and truly picked. For Uncle Benjamin could be trusted implicity to tell the truth; had he not been at Trinity College in Dublin, with the dean himself? Together they had studied, together they had in due course been ordained into the Church of Ireland. Whereupon Uncle Benjamin, full of quirks even then, had immediately decided the Church was not after all for him. He had declined a curacy and had gone to sea as an apprentice.

Having gone to sea exceptionally late in life—he was then twenty-three—he had been in a curious position *vis-à-vis* his shipmates, and not from the viewpoint of age alone—a parson in the half-deck was to say the least a rarity and not a welcome one among a generation of seamen who regarded all parsons as Jonahs when aboard a ship at sea. However, he had survived handsomely and in the end had caught up with time. At thirty-six he had been made master in the Conway Shire Line and had remained in command until the age of sixty-seven when he had, as he put it, swallowed the anchor and, still a bachelor, had gone to live in Chesterfield with a sister. That had been five years ago. He filled in his retirement by taking part in services at his local church, clad in cassock and surplice, for, having of course never been unfrocked, he was still, when he wished it, Captain the Reverend Benjamin Brand, BA, Master Mariner.

He and the dean had always remained friends—close, if not by continual physical proximity, then by correspondence interspersed by occasional meetings when the captain had been on leave with time to visit an old crony in the West of Ireland. And it was the yarns spun by Uncle Benjamin that had sown the seed of adventure in Tom's mind.

As the dean had known perfectly well. 'So, you see,' he grumbled, 'it's entirely your fault, Benjamin. *Entirely.'*

'Really,—'

'Even, if I may say so, Benjamin, to the extent of his being apparently against any idea of the navy. You were always somewhat sarcastic about Her Majesty's ships as I recall.' The dean peered over the top of a pair of *pince-nez* and pursed his whiskered lips. 'Were you not?'

Uncle Benjamin slapped the arm of his chair. 'Damme, you still have the look about you of a rat peering out of a ball of oakum! You don't change, Desmond me boy. But to get back to what you were saying, now. Sarcastic, was I? By God I was,' he said with feeling. His white side-whiskers quivered with emotion around the square, weatherbeaten face. 'A damned lazy lot, Desmond, damned lazy, not to say bone idle. And pompous! Set of damn fools if you ask my opinion! Not,' he added, 'that there haven't been some fine exceptions.'

The dean raised an eyebrow. 'Nelson?' he suggested tongue-in-cheek.

'Nelson,' Captain Brand agreed. 'Nothing against him at all. A great admiral and a fine seaman. Did I ever tell you, my own father met him once—'

'Yes, Benjamin, you did tell me.'

'Ah. Ah, well. It's a long time ago now, of course.' The old seadog lifted his whiskey glass and drank pleasurably. Then he took a pinch of snuff, sneezed mightily for a while, and at last said, 'Now. About the boy. Is he set on this, Desmond, really set?'

'He seems to be,' the dean answered, looking disconsolate.

'And why not, why not?' Captain Brand's considerable jaw was thrust forward. 'Good God, man, don't look so damned dismal about it!' He gave a sudden rumbling chuckle; and drank more whiskey. 'Dismal Desmond...by the great Lord Harry, but that fits to a T.' He shook with suppressed laughter.

'Do be serious,' the dean snapped.

'Very well, old friend, I shall be serious. Pray tell me, what are your objections to the boy going to sea?'

For answer, Dean Chatto looked first around the study. Like the Board Room of Porter Holt, his walls were hung with portraits of earlier generations, in this case Chattos all plus the Chatto wives.

There was much ancestry, going back to the time of Queen Elizabeth and commencing on the north wall with Bishop Chatto. On another wall hung General Sir Gervaise Chatto, the dean's own ancestor, descended from a brother of Bishop Chatto... Following the dean's gaze, Captain Brand guessed what was to come. He was right. The dean said irritably, 'It's not a gentleman's life, Benjamin, I don't care what you say.'

'I've not said anything yet. As a matter of fact, I agree with you. It's not a gentleman's life.' Captain Brand blew out a long breath like a whiskey-laden gale. 'Oh, damme, Desmond, I know you backwards! Always were a dreadful snob. Of course it's not a gentleman's life. Can you tell me what is?'

'Well...' the dean said.

'Quite—you're stumped when it comes to the point. I'll answer my own question: nothing is a gentleman's life—except doing absolutely nothing whatsoever, which I call a mortal sin against the Holy Ghost for did not our Lord—'

'The Church,' the Dean broke in somewhat desperately.

'The Church, is it? Plenty of fellows

of no family are getting livings today as you must know. The Church is no guarantee of gentle birth. But does that matter? To me, my dear Desmond, the term "a gentleman's life" has no very precise meaning. What counts, surely to goodness, is what a man himself *is*. If he is a gentleman, that is enough. He carries his *life*, if you wish to speak of it, with him wherever he goes and whatever he does. Now.' The old man sat forward and spoke very earnestly. 'I agree there are plenty of very common fellows amongst the afterguard of our merchantmen—very rough and ready, with no parentage within your terms of reference. Nevertheless, they are mostly good fellows. *Men*—leading manly lives. And don't you see, there are plenty of the others as well. Doctors' sons, lawyers' sons, even parsons' sons. Yes. Especially parsons' sons I assure you. I believe it's an escape. But the real point is, the life appeals to a wide cross-section of our society—on account of the element of manliness and adventure which rightly overrides the lesser consideration of class. In my view there is something extra special about a gentleman who chooses the sea life in the merchant ships. It's a *clean* life and an honest one.' He added, 'Do Tom the world of good.'

The dean stiffened indignantly. 'What do you mean?'

Captain Brand's answer was short. 'Boy's getting soft.'

'Oh, rubbish! Utter rubbish. Why, goodness me, he's out sailing this very minute!'

'That's not the point. Point is, he was his mother's boy, Desmond, and you must face it—and I'm not apologizing, so help me God, when a boy's future's in the balance. Of course I respect your feelings—none more so. Effie, God rest her, was a saint and at the risk of sounding of popery I'll be the first to state it and defend her claim. But saints are not necessarily good for boys and neither are their memories. The sea *will* do him good. It'll make a man of him. You mark my words—a man.'

'Or the opposite, Benjamin. I've heard you say before, quite often, that the sea can either make a man or break him, and—'

'Aye,' Captain Brand agreed with a keen look at the dean, 'or break him, yes. And I still believe it's worth the trying.'

Later in the course of that visit Uncle Benjamin, talking at length and privately to Tom Chatto, had used those words again, with much emphasis, and Tom had sensed that the old sailor was testing him out. A determination formed within him, a determination that over the next weeks became almost a fixation, to prove to Uncle Benjamin that he could succeed come what may.

So there could be no backing out now.

# CHAPTER 4

'Rouse out, there—rouse out! A-a-a-all hands! Every mother's son o'yer...show a leg, the sun's a-burning yer eyes out...'

'Bloody liar,' came Jim Wales' voice, thick with sleep. There was a heavy thump on the bulkhead of the half-deck, a blow from an iron belaying-pin, and a moment later the door was flung open and a face looked in. Wales yawned, put a leg from the blanket and said, 'Good morning, bosun.'

'A good morning to *you*, young'un, and that'll do for the small talk if you don't mind. Today we leave England, home and beauty and the Old Man's up already—so out o'yer bunks the lot o'youse.'

The bosun disappeared, leaving the door open behind him. A spatter of rain blew in on the wind, eddying along the narrow passage between half-deck and petty officers' accommodation. Wales cursed, and slammed it shut. Tom, peering from his blanket, saw the senior apprentice reach for the oil-lamp and light it, for it was still dark. The lamp lit and smoking badly, Wales tweaked the blankets off the other three. 'Out,' he said sharply. 'You heard what O'Connor said. Let's show willing...there's plenty to be done before the tug's alongside.'

Tom emerged, shivering. The half-deck was icy and the opened door hadn't helped. He made a grab for his shirt and trousers and pulled them on fast over the vest and pants in which he'd slept—thanks to a warning from Uncle Benjamin he hadn't brought a nightshirt; to the cruel scorn of Wales and Allan, Horatio Mainprice had. There had been ribaldry about teddy bears and hot-water bottles, and mater coming along soon to tuck him up. Mainprice had turned in almost in tears and was still sulking. Wales looked Tom up and down. 'Don't you wash in Ireland?' he asked.

'Of course, but it's too cold to—'

Wales seized his arm. The senior apprentice on sailing day was a different young man from the day before. 'Cold? You'll not know the meaning of the word, Chatto, till we're wallowing off Cape Stiff, searching for a shift of wind to take us round. In the meantime, I don't like dirty company. Off with your shirt—and quick about it. You as well,' he added to Mainprice. 'Get that sissy thing off and your trousers on. This morning you'll wash in the galley. After today it'll be the deck pump outside.'

'Pump? *Outside?*' Mainprice obviously couldn't believe his ears. He looked amazed, as if he had a lunatic to deal with.

'That's what I said—'

'A pump to wash with, yet you have a decent WC—'

'Heads to you. And don't you argue with me, young Mainprice.' Wales loomed over him, fists clenched. He lifted one of them and waved it in Mainprice's face. 'See that? It has a name. Learn it. It's called Hospital. The other's Sudden

Death. Understand? You don't answer back aboard a ship. Now—get along to the galley. It's fresh water today. From the time we clear the basin, the pumps'll be connected to the seawater.'

'Salt water...to wash in?'

Wales grinned. 'Salt and cold. Didn't nanny tell you, you wouldn't get a fire to dress by? Out, the three of you.'

There was just one basin in the galley and it was filled with warmish, dirty water: others had been there before them. Mainprice recoiled like a virgin, and the cook, Joshua Leggatt, laughed loudly. As he stirred a concoction in a huge iron pan on the stove he said in a mincing voice, ' 'Is Lordship not satisfied wiv 'is bleedin' 'ip-bath, then?'

'I'm not putting a finger in that,' Horatio Mainprice said with a snort. 'Filthy muck.'

Josh Leggatt came away from his stove. 'You'll follow the custom o' this 'ere bloody barque, *mister,* or I'll pour the lot down yer perishin' little neck, so 'elp me. Don't you know fresh water's a bloody luxury aboard a ship—even in port, where it 'as to be paid for?'

It was a horrible business for newly

joined apprentices and Tom thought with longing of the school holidays when the deanery housemaids had brought cans of piping hot water to the bedroom wash-stands or hip-baths; the *Pass of Drumochter* was worse even than school. Washed as briefly as possible under Slushy's scornful eye, they dashed back into the half-deck and finished dressing, pulling on seaboots and oilskins and souwesters. Tom was scarcely ready when the commotion began on deck, starting with the shouts of the bosun and the Second Mate, Mr Underwood. Tom heard the hands tumbling out from the fo'c'sle accommodation and moving along the deck, and then the thump of blocks and other deck gear. Soon the voice of Mr Patience could be heard hazeing the men. There was a real bite in his voice now, a sound close to hate.

Wales, going out on deck with Tom, explained that sailing day had its own special problem.

'Drink,' he said. 'Most of the fo'c'sle gang'll have spent every penny in the public houses last night, saying a fond farewell to England. They'll all be feeling like death warmed up at the moment. It's

Patience's job to bring 'em alive-o again.'

Tom scanned the men as they shambled past. They would look a murderous enough bunch, many of them, at the best of times and this morning, as he could see in the increasing but still grey light of the dawn, they did indeed look like very death. Their faces were white, their eyes bleary, their hands shook as they laid hold of ropes or simply clung for support to bulwarks and ratlines. If they should be ordered aloft before the liquor fumes had cleared from their heads, surely instinct alone could save their lives. One man was violently and messily sick at Tom's feet and he started back in disgust.

'What's up, then?' the man demanded hoarsely. 'Too bloody delicate to see such...young whippersnapper.'

Tom said nothing as the sick white face was thrust close to his own and the vomit-laden breath struck him with the sour stench of old beer and rum. But the man had been seen from the poop. The First Mate's voice roared out: 'O'Connor! See to that man pronto.'

They waited for the Mersey tide. The morning had worn on to a dull, dirty yellow-grey by the time Captain Theodore Landon climbed the ladder running up through the poop-deck hatch. Behind him came an officer of Her Majesty's Customs, an officer of the waterguard who had examined the jerque note issued after the inward cargo had been discharged and the vessel rummaged for contraband, and who had now cleared her for foreign. Behind this official came the mud-pilot who would take the ship off the berth and through the locks to clear the basin, after which he would hand over to the river-pilot. On the starboard side a steam tug was seen approaching through the grey overcast, moving slowly across the basin for the outward-bounder. As the tug drifted up to lie off the bow, there was a hail from her bridge, answered by the mud-pilot who then nodded at Captain Landon.

Landon caught the eye of the First Mate. 'Single up, if you please, Mr Patience.'

'Aye, aye, sir.' Patience picked up a megaphone and shouted through it. 'Mr Underwood—cast off second headrope and sternrope, cast off breasts.' He turned to Landon. 'Springs, sir?'

'Let them go, Mr Patience.'

The megaphone came up again. 'Let go

springs fore and aft...stand by for'ard to take the tug's line.'

Patience lowered the megaphone and made his way quickly down from the poop and along the waist to the bow. As the echoes of his strong voice died away there was a curious quietness, a sad and melancholy quietness Tom Chatto found it as he bent to the after spring with two of the hands and heaved it inboard. There was a splash from farther aft as the shore gang let go the sternrope from its bollard, and the eye slid from the dock into the murky water. The ship's crew brought it in, hand over hand, dripping, and coiled it down on the deck. With only one headrope and one sternrope to hold her now, the *Pass of Drumochter* waited for the order that would let the last lines go. The helmsman, standing stolid behind the wheel, chewed on a plug of tobacco, the dark juice running down from a corner of his mouth, while he kept an eye lifting on the masts and yards—kept an eye lifting from sheer force of habit, for until the great sails were loosed along the yards there was little point in looking aloft; it was just something that became second nature to any sailorman. The helmsman's thoughts were with his wife, who would at that moment be at work in a Merseyside mill; the helmsman was one of the very few married men among the fo'c'sle hands. One of the very few in the whole ship, in fact, for, apart from Captain Landon and Mr Patience, the only others were Bosun O'Connor and the carpenter.

The helmsman was still thinking of his wife when a heaving-line was sent snaking through the air from the tug, to be caught in the eyes of the ship by a seaman who brought it through a fairlead to the bitts. Behind it came a heavier line, then the tow proper, a heavy hemp hawser sparkling with rain and basin water. When the tow had been made fast a report was made to the poop and Landon turned to the customs official.

'Well now, Mr Merryweather, I am ready to proceed, if you'll be so good as to step ashore now.'

They shook hands. 'A safe voyage, Captain, and a prosperous one.'

'Thank you indeed.' Like a gracious old lion, Captain Landon bowed his head. The customs man made his way to the brow, which was brought in immediately after he had crossed to the dockside. The mud-pilot spoke to the Captain and the order was passed for the remaining ropes to be let go. When the lines fell slack and were brought inboard the last links with the land had virtually gone. Now there were just the locks ahead and then they would be away across the seas for Sydney.

There was no one to see them go, bar the small unberthing party and a few circling seagulls crying eerily as they swooped upon the trucks of the masts or skimmed the water for garbage, and a disinterested watchman looking from the after rails of the ship in the next berth; even the customs man had made a dash through the rain for a warehouse. A departure from Liverpool docks on a 12,000-mile run across the world was too ordinary an occurrence to excite any special interest; the *Pass of Drumochter* was merely one of a dozen ships that would leave the Mersey River that day for foreign ports to carry the British flag across the seas; but to Tom Chatto it was a unique occasion and filled with all kinds of emotions from fear to pride. It was the start of a new life, of a career that would take him many times to the ends of the earth, through every one of the world's seas, to as yet undreamed of experiences and loves and hates, personal battles and stormy waters and quiet interludes. Even as he worked under the bosun's direction and the alert eyes of the First and Second Mates, he was somehow aware of all this, aware that not only was the die well and truly cast now but also that he would come back to the Mersey a man, and a totally different person too. Uncle Benjamin had been right. Nothing, Tom knew instinctively, would ever be quite the same again. Childhood, boyhood, even his youth, were all behind him now.

They passed through the locks behind the tug, turned in the stream and headed outwards for the mouth of the Mersey and Liverpool Bay. The air was cold and damp and there was still a drizzle but there was no hint yet of any wind and it was clearly going to be necessary to tow right out, perhaps even as far as the Skerries.

The water was dead flat, oily-looking, pocked by the rain. Tom watched the Liverpool and Birkenhead buildings slide past and away, slowly. The hands stood ready by the tug's line and the braces, so that the yards could be hauled round in a trice once the sails had been shaken out and the fullest advantage taken of the first sniff of a breeze, when they would dispense with the tug. It cost good money to take the tug and pilot too far, and every sovereign counted in the windjammers' life- battle against the steam monsters with their belching smoke and dirt. To that extent every man was behind the Owners: none of the crew wished to see sail vanish from the seas.

Landon kept a close eye on the sky and the surface of the water, and on the Red Ensign hanging limp from the mizzen peak. At the first sign of wind his order would send the men aloft to swarm up the ratlines and out along the footropes to loose the sails—the sails that Tom Chatto and Horatio Mainprice had yet to learn to identify by name at a glance, along with the names and precise functions of every single one of the hundreds of ropes that criss-crossed overhead, running from deck to masts, to yards, from mast to mast and back again, to sails and booms and bowsprit. Tom would have to learn the difference between standing and running rigging, between guys and braces and downhauls, clewlines and gaskets and buntlines, garnets and halliards and sheets to name a few. The names of the sails alone—skysails, royals, topgallants, upper and lower topsails, courses...spanker, jigger staysail, foretopmast staysail, jibs...it was a kind of nightmare for anyone until the whole lot gelled in the mind to become instinctive.

The sudden rasp of the First Mate's voice made Tom jump.

'Damn your eyes, boy—you're not here to dream about home, you're here to work.' Patience's object, it seemed, was Horatio Mainprice, who was resting his weary back against the fo'c'sle guardrail. 'Do you understand me, boy?'

'Yes, sir. But there's nothing to do, is there?'

*'Nothing to do?'* Even Mr Patience was taken aback; he gaped like a landed fish. 'Nothing to do...aboard a sailing ship under way? And stand up straight when you speak to me, boy!'

Mainprice straightened, his mouth thinning, his eyes not meeting the Mate's hard stare. Patience said in an ominously quiet voice, 'Go to the half-deck this instant, Mainprice. Fetch your toothbrush.'

'Fetch what?'

'You heard me.' The Mate's fists clenched.

Mainprice went, bad-temperedly, showing his disdain in his supercilious walk. He came back with the toothbrush. Still there was no wind. Patience said, 'Now, boy. The starboard anchor's dirty—isn't it?'

Mainprice went across to where the anchor was catted outside the guardrail, secure to the clump cathead. He made a business of looking, then turned and said, 'I don't think so. It looks perfectly clean to me.' He added, 'Sir.'

'You say it's clean. It doesn't look clean to me. Look again.'

Mainprice did so. 'I still say it's clean.'

'So you're calling me a liar, boy?'

Mainprice looked startled. 'Oh no, sir!'

'But you are—if you say that anchor's clean. I say it's dirty. Well?'

Mainprice's gaze flickered around the fo'c'sle. No one said a word, but all the men, while contriving to look busy, were grinning. Mainprice took a deep breath and said sullenly, 'All right, it's dirty.'

'Sir.'

'Sir.'

'It's not only dirty, it's filthy. Absolutely filthy. Isn't it?'

'Yes, sir.'

'So now tell me again: what is the starboard anchor, *Mister* Mainprice?'

There was a pause; the apprentice's face was flaming when he muttered, 'Absolutely filthy, sir.'

Patience grinned and said, 'I'm glad you agree. So clean it. Scrub it. *With the toothbrush.*'

As Mainprice climbed mutinously over the guardrail Patience turned to one of the older hands, a man with a brown, wizened face like a monkey's and no teeth. He said, 'Finney, you can give us a send-off. We'll have a capstan shanty...just while Mister Mainprice learns that when I say a thing's dirty it bloody well drips filth and corruption.'

'Yessir,' Finney said, and scurried down the fo'c'sle ladder. He was back within a couple of minutes carrying a fiddle. He sat himself on the capstan and drew a bow across the strings in a preliminary movement. He grinned his toothless grin at the First Mate.

'Play, then,' Patience ordered. 'And everybody sing.'

76

As they waited for the breeze to come and relieve them of the tug smoking fussily ahead of them, drawing them away from England, towards the open sea and the long haul south to Cape Horn, Able Seaman Finney played and the crew sang in strong, clear voices that were accustomed to call across wide spaces and into the teeth of gales; and the finest voice of them all, oddly, was that of Mr Patience, who sang in a full-throated bass that would have done credit to any professional singer. And for the first time Tom listened to the words that ever after would stay in his memory, stay there long after such shanties had become things of the romantic past, dead and buried and forgotten along with the grey ghosts of the legions of seafarers who had sung them in all the ports of the world where the British flag had waved:

'And it's home, dearie, home! Oh, it's home I want to be,
But my tops'ls are hoisted, and I must out to sea;
While the oak, and the ash, and the bonnie birchen tree
They're all a-growing green in the North Countree...'

To Tom's surprise, he saw the Mate's face working with an emotion that was very close to tears. He shook his head in sheer wonderment.

## CHAPTER 5

The wind came, not much but enough, as the *Pass of Drumochter* was coming up towards Point Lynas in Anglesey and standing well clear of the land. Captain Landon was the first to react; he brought the hands to on the instant. Through his megaphone he called for'ard to the Mate.

'Mr Patience, the wind—nor'-nor'-easterly. Make sail, if you please, and let go the tug.'

Another call through the megaphone brought the pilot boat alongside and a man ran to lower a Jacob's ladder. Patience, and the sound of his voice, seemed to be everywhere. As the tug was cast off from the bitts and swung away to make back into the Mersey, the bulk of the seamen were swarming up the ratlines to lay out along the yards; those remaining on deck stood by the sheets and braces. Jim Wales was one of the first to start climbing, leading some of the hands to the foretop and beyond, going out himself along the thin, swaying footrope of the fore topgallant yard; Ted Allan led another party to the mainmast. Tom and Horatio Mainprice were gathered up in the wake of the First Mate and sent to the sheets and braces on the port and the starboard side respectively.

Tom found himself working under Mr Underwood, the Second Mate. Until the great sails had been set overhead there was little for him to do but watch and learn. Captain Landon was making all sail to the royals in order to take the fullest advantage of what wind there was to carry him off to a good start to the Bishop Rock. The turn of the hands at the braces would come when the Master started to trim the yards to the wind.

There was more shouting from the deck when the unfurled sails were seen to be ready for setting. Patience passed the order for the clew of the main course to be hauled out first by the sheet, and Tom found himself sweating on the end of the rope as the biggest sail of all was hauled to the main yard. In quick succession, working from bottom to top, the rest of the canvas was hauled out, and then the yards were hoisted to their positions by the halliards. As the sails filled, Landon trimmed them to the wind, and Tom was sent to tail onto the lee mainbrace to haul the yard to the proper angle of trim. It was efficiently done and soon the *Pass of Drumochter* was going ahead for the Skerries and the turn south into the Irish Sea, moving along through only slightly ruffled water at four knots.

When all the gear had been overhauled and the decks cleared up, all hands were called aft for the port and starboard watches to be picked, and this done the hands, except for the watch now on deck, were sent below to make short if belated work of Joshua Leggatt's cooking efforts—cooking that had been interrupted by the operation of setting the sails, for 'all sail' was a job for all hands and the cook, and Leggatt had in fact been one of the men tending the halliards on Tom's side of the ship.

When the fall-out from stations came Mr Underwood had a word with Tom Chatto.

'How's it feel,' he asked cheerfully, 'to be at sea?'

'Fine, sir, thank you.'

'You were a shade ham-fisted at the braces, but you'll do better next time. Remember one thing: never, if you want to live, put a foot in a bight of rope. If what's on the other end of the rope should take charge and run away, well, it's likely you'd be playing a harp.'

There were, it seemed, many things to remember aboard a ship if you wanted to go on living. Underwood sounded another note of warning. 'Don't make the mistake,' he said, 'of thinking you've seen everything. Today it was easy; in a gale of wind, or a heavy sea after a gale—it isn't. It's a very different kettle of fish then and it's different again when there's ice on the rigging, as you'll be finding out.'

That afternoon Mr Patience ordered the new apprentices aloft, just to try it out under the direction of Jim Wales. The Mate issued another warning. 'Never hold on by the ratlines. You have to use them as your foothold, of course, but you trust your hand-grip to the shrouds themselves.'

Mainprice, oddly enough, took to what was an ordeal like a duck to water, swarming with confidence up the shrouds from the waist, reaching the maintop in no time at all. Wales was pleased. He looked down, waiting for Tom Chatto to join them on the small platform just above the main yard. Tom came up slowly, holding tight to the shrouds, feeling carefully for each foothold on what he felt to be a terrifyingly limp ladder of tarred one-and-a-half-inch hemp to form the ratlines, his body flattened against it for greater security. When he was a little way below the platform he stuck fast, staring at the outward-slanting futtock shrouds.

'Hurry it up,' Wales called down. He sounded impatient; there was a snigger from Horatio Mainprice. 'Damn it all,' Wales said, 'it's a dead flat calm, young Chatto. What are you going to do when there's a forty-knot gale tearing at you?'

'I'll be all right in a moment,' Tom said desperately. He looked down, although he'd been warned not to, and he nearly gave up. The deck seemed miles away, with the men of the watch like puppets and the sea creaming away astern from either side of the bowsprit. He hung on by an effort of will. Above him the main shrouds led through a hole, known as the lubber's hole, to the maintop. It was the easy way but he dare not take it, must not be labelled a lubber on his first day; seamen used the futtock shrouds. Leaning outwards and backwards, the futtock shrouds led from the shrouds proper to the outer edges of the maintop, one from each side. Feeling the sick thump of his heart, Tom reached out, leaning backwards over the deck far below, his body, with gravity now acting upon its whole length and not just through his feet, held by fingers and slipping toes alone.

Doggedly, he climbed.

Just when he felt on the point of blacking out he reached the maintop and, thankfully, heaved himself over onto the platform, from which more ratlines extended heavenward.

Wales clapped him on the shoulder. 'Well enough done,' he said. 'Slow—but you made it. It'll not be so bad the next time, I promise you. If you'd gone through the lubber's hole this first time, you'd never have done it at all.' He added, 'How d'you feel about going up the topmast now?'

Tom looked up. From the maintop the ratlines climbed much more vertically, much closer to the mast itself. There was a wind now, coming in gusts, alternately plucking at Tom's body and letting it fall slack again, so that there was a difficulty in adjusting his balance on the narrow platform. The slatting of the sails and the rattle of the gear added to his feeling of insecurity.

He took a grip on himself. 'I'll give it a go,' he said.

'That's the spirit. I'll go first, you next, then you, nipper.'

Wales reached up for the shrouds and started the climb, taking it with practised ease. Fearfully Tom followed, every step on the ratlines an effort. The higher he went, the stronger the wind seemed to become. Looking outboard he saw the small white crests forming along the tops of shallow waves; he heard the sigh and hum of the wind through the rigging. Eyes wide, body flattened as before to the ratlines, he went on. Reaching the topmasthead at last he saw the shrouds that led almost vertically up the topgallantmast; and above, the bare pole to the royal masthead and the truck. Wales, moving onto the topgallantmast, said, 'Hang on and get your breath back.'

He continued climbing himself, easily, almost gracefully, with the full confidence that came with experience. Tom clung to the shrouds, feeling a terrible urge to let go. He looked out to sea, to starboard, towards a smudge of land visible on the horizon as a low, dark line with hills beyond: Ireland. He didn't know just where they were at that moment, but somewhere to starboard might lie the Wicklow Hills. Once, not so many years ago, he had spent a happy holiday in the Wicklow Hills with his mother and his sister. That had in fact been the last holiday before the accident that had killed his mother. He felt a wave of sadness, of vain regret for a life that was gone. He was still thinking of the past when Jim Wales came down and told him curtly to wake up and climb back to the deck. He was once more on the comparative security of the maintop before he fully realized he'd done it, and he felt enough confidence to go over the futtock shrouds, although he had a nasty moment when his legs, swinging out into space, couldn't find the ratlines.

Back on deck Wales said, 'You didn't do so badly, either of you.' That was all;

but Tom knew the senior apprentice was pleased.

That afternoon as the wind freshened the *Pass of Drumochter* made fair speed down towards the Bishop Rock. Tom and Horatio Mainprice were set to the wearisome task of cleaning down, a never-ending chore aboard a ship. Later in the voyage they would be given instruction in seamanship and navigation, but it was early days yet.

At an average speed of a spanking seven knots, the *Pass of Drumochter* raised the Bishop light at two bells in the last dogwatch the following day and when his ship was abeam of the rock the Captain set a course that would take him into the South Atlantic to pass some four hundred and fifty miles to the westward of the Canaries. The first port of call was to be Recife in Pernambuco, Brazil. This first leg of the voyage would, by Landon's estimate, take them thirty days.

It was during the forenoon watch on the morning after they had taken their departure from the Bishop Rock that Tom Chatto made up his mind that this, his first voyage, would be his last.

He would desert the ship at Recife rather than face one more day of seasickness. Currently he wished only to die, and to do so in the comparative peace of the scuppers into which, at the very end of his strength, he had fallen, quite unmindful of the seas that swilled around him to be discharged overboard through the washports. His stomach, sore and empty from continual retching, felt as if it contained all the fires of hell concentrated into one terrible globule of molten lead. He was shivering uncontrollably and his face was like a sheet of parchment when Mr Patience found him and ordered him, roughly, to get to his feet and be quick about it.

He rose unsteadily. Before he had been able to get a grip on the bulwarks the deck gave a sudden lurch as a gust of wind laid her over, and Tom lost his balance on the slippery planks and crashed back into the scuppers.

Mr Patience, whose breath reeked of the tobacco he was chewing, bent and seized him. Tom was dragged upright.

'Keep on your feet, boy. There's work to be done. No skrim-shaking's allowed aboard any ship that has me for Mate. The sooner you learn that, the better it'll be for you. Now—get you to the galley. Leggatt has work for idle hands.'

Tom stared glassily back at the Mate, his stomach heaving with bile. His sou'wester had gone overboard; the wind, sighing through halliards and shrouds and guys, plucked at his oilskin, held around the waist by a length of tarred spunyarn. He took a step towards the galley, his head swimming. Patience moved around ahead of him, his big face hard, lips working as he chewed the tobacco. A dark brown drool started from one corner of his mouth. He took Tom's shoulders and held him steady, then with one hand he grabbed his face and pinched his cheeks until the mouth came open. And then, with the sudden speed of a striking snake, he spat, directing a long stream of tobacco juice into Tom's open mouth; after which he held him with a hand beneath his chin, clamping his mouth tight shut.

'You'll never be so sick again in all your life at sea, as you're feeling now,' he said. 'You've had the worst. Remember that. It's for your own good, boy.'

He turned and walked away along the deck. Tom, his whole body hot and cold alternately, rushed for the bulwarks and hung over the side, bringing his very heart up. The First Mate watched him from the bows, but didn't interfere again. Five minutes later Tom staggered away from the bulwarks and lurched along to the galley, where Joshua Leggatt had also been watching.

Tom muttered, 'The Mate says you've a job for me, Mr Leggatt.'

'Never mind the mister, just call me what I'm known as and that's Slushy. The cook, poor sod, is always called Slushy.' He turned away to his stove, while Tom strove to disregard the smell of cooking. 'And here's the first job of work,' Leggatt went on a moment later, turning round with an iron mug in his hand. 'Drink that and be thankful. Put it down fast and you'll feel a lot better, lad.'

It was a tot of rum, strong Jamaica, with a dash of hot water. It seemed to work. By the time Tom, sitting out on deck with a bucket, had peeled the potatoes for dinner things looked more cheerful. Leggatt, attending to his cooking, said, 'The Mate knows what he's about, none better. I see 'im work that one before now, and it's always been successful. He's not as bad as you're thinking.' He stirred a great iron pan of thin-looking soup. 'It's a great life when you get yer sea legs, young 'un.'

It began to seem more hopeful that afternoon when the sun broke through and the clouds rolled away to reveal a bright blue sky. The sun sparkled on the waters, bringing all the colours of the rainbow to the spray that was flung back from the bow as the *Pass of Drumochter* cut through the waves. There were small breaking crests all around to relieve the deep blue that reached to the horizons. At six bells in the twelve to four watch, smoke was seen ahead by the lookout and reported to the officer of the watch on the poop. Captain Landon was called, and came up with his wife. They were joined by Mr Patience, who was politely attentive to Mrs Landon, an attitude that sat somewhat uneasily on the First Mate, and Tom watched in some surprise.

Landon climbed into the lower mizzen rigging and put his telescope to his eye. 'Six steam men-o'-war, Mr Patience,' he said after a while. 'Most likely a battle squadron of the Channel Fleet.' He remained in the rigging until the men-o'-war had come closer and then, stepping down, announced that he had been mistaken: they were not line-of-battle ships but armoured cruisers. The ships, steaming in line ahead, swept majestically down the port side of the windjammer, with the flagship wearing at her main truck the red St George's Cross on a white ground, with one red ball in the upper canton next the staff, which indicated the presence of a vice-admiral.

'Mr Patience, dip the ensign, if you please.'

The Mate, with a fleeting glance at Mrs Landon, moved to the signal halliard and brought the Red Ensign down to the dip. As each of the Queen's ships passed, she dipped her own ensign in acknowledgement of the courtesy, then ran it close up again to the mizzen peak. When the last of the warships had passed the Mate brought the Red Ensign back to its position and made fast the halliard.

'A fine sight,' Landon said, looking aft towards the line of vessels and the disturbed wakes left by their pounding screws. Turning, he caught the eye of Tom Chatto and of Horatio Mainprice. 'Can either of you lads tell me anything about those ships?' he asked gruffly.

'I can, sir,' Mainprice said. He stepped

forward. 'The flagship is Her Majesty's Ship *Warspite,* of 8,400 tons, and the next in line is the *Imperieuse* of the same tonnage. Both have partial armoured belts ten inches thick, sir, with waterline armour, steel-protected decks and conning towers, with their heavy guns mounted along the upper decks in turrets. They're comparatively new ships, sir. The others, slightly older, are the *Amphion,* the *Severn,* the *Iris* and the *Mercury*...these not being armoured, sir, and having gun-shields instead of turrets.' He spoke pedantically and somewhat unctuously, and Landon smiled.

'You know a great deal, young man. Perhaps you can tell me the name of the officer commanding?'

'I can, sir. The squadron's under the command of Vice-Admiral Sir William Rivers.'

'Indeed,' Landon said drily.

'Yes, sir. The admiral is a friend of my family. I've been aboard his flagship.'

'A fine vessel no doubt, and a fine service,' Landon said. He paused. 'This is perhaps a suitable time to mention one thing to both of you youngsters. You are no doubt aware of the existence of the

Royal Naval Reserve. This force has now been in being for nearly thirty years. You will find Porter Holt not sorry to see a number of RNR officers aboard their ships, and they're generous in allowing leave to comply with the qualifying service aboard the warships that is an annual requirement. You would do well to bear this in mind.'

Mainprice said, 'Yes, sir,' but offered no further comment. The Captain nodded in dismissal and turned away. Taking his wife's arm he stared after the homeward-bound squadron, hurrying back to wives and sweethearts after what had probably been a brief visit to Gibraltar. Landon gave an involuntary sigh, not for himself since he carried his home with him, but for his brother masters and officers who were not so fortunate. The Queen's navy had its shore appointments and its short cruises to compensate for its long foreign commissions; but for the blue-water merchantmen every voyage was a long foreign commission, world without end, from apprenticeship to retirement.

Walking for'ard from the poop, Tom asked Mainprice if he'd known about the RNR.

'Of course,' Mainprice answered snappishly. 'The old fool...wasting his breath.' He turned to look at the vanishing naval squadron; he seemed about to speak again, then a sly look came over his face and he turned away.

Three days later, when the *Pass of Drumochter* was bowling south under clear skies and before a fresh wind, Force 5 on the Beaufort Scale, with all sail set still, Mr Patience noticed that the canvas cover of the lifeboat, set in chocks amidships, was improperly secured. He sent for the bosun.

'Explain *that* if you can,' he said shortly.

O'Connor scratched at his cheek. He said, 'All was well when I checked before sailing, sir.'

'How long before sailing?'

O'Connor shrugged. 'Just the day previous.'

'And you've noticed nothing since?' There was, in truth, little to be seen beyond a loosening of the rope through the eyelets in the tarpaulin; but Patience had an eye for any omission. 'Not good enough. If such occurs again, O'Connor, you'll not be bosun of this ship or of any of the company's ships for much longer. You'll recollect I was not pleased with you last voyage. I'll not warn you again.'

O'Connor's face had whitened and his fingers seemed to be shaking. 'Aye, sir. I'm sorry, sir. It'll not happen again. I'll see to it immediately.'

'Do so.' The Mate turned away and walked for'ard, gazing aloft at the sails straining at the cringles. Bosun O'Connor, scowling at the Mate's back, began tautening up the tarpaulin. Tom Chatto, busy nearby with a brass-polishing cloth, found his eye caught by the glint of the sun on metal through the small gap that had been noticed by Mr Patience.

He saw something move inside the lifeboat. He could have sworn it was a hand, and that the hand was holding a pistol. If he was right, they had a stowaway aboard. Tom, having to all intents and purposes seen nothing, went on with his work. Then, as the bosun, hauling the rope through the brass eyelets, finished securing the tarpaulin and closed the gap, Tom put a finger to his lips and drew O'Connor along the deck. 'There's a man in the boat,' he whispered. 'I think he's got a pistol.'

O'Connor was startled. '*What?* Are you sure of this, lad?'

'Almost sure. He doesn't know I've seen him. I suppose we'd better report to Mr Patience.'

'Wait,' the bosun said quickly, putting a hand on Tom's arm. 'Aside o' you and me...no one knows of this.'

'No.'

'Now, young Mister Chatto...' The bosun's expression and tone grew crafty. 'That's the way it'd best be left. Just for now that is. We'll not report the matter. D'you understand, lad?'

'But...' Tom floundered. 'I'm sorry, but I don't understand. Surely a stowaway has to be reported.'

'Only once we know for sure,' O'Connor answered mysteriously. He looked around: there was no one within earshot. 'No false alarms, lad. And if there is a man there, and he's armed...why, there'll be danger to life. It's my job to see to it, but not yet. We'll wait for darkness, and then the business will be the easier, and much safer. D'ye understand now?'

Tom shook his head in doubt; but the bosun was the bosun and an experienced man. O'Connor went on, 'Not a word of this to a soul. Ye'll promise me that, lad.' He was still holding onto Tom's arm and now he increased the pressure, staring sternly at the first-voyager. 'I'd never wish to cause danger to any shipmate, nor, I think, would you. So keep your own counsel, boy, and give me the promise that you will.'

Tom had to assume that the bosun must know his duty. He gave the promise. He was troubled about this during the rest of that day, a fact that Jim Wales noticed when the off-watch apprentices were at supper in the half-deck.

'What's the trouble, young Chatto?'

Tom said, 'Oh—nothing. Why?'

'You're looking too thoughtful by half. If you've run up against any difficulties, you'd do better to get 'em off your chest.'

A promise was a promise. 'No, it's nothing. Really it isn't.'

That night it was Tom's turn for the midnight to four a.m watch as understudy to the Second Mate. Pulling on his clothes when roused out, rubbing the sleep from his eyes, he went out on deck into a cold and rising wind, a wind that was bellying the sails out from their clews with the yards braced square. Going aft to the poop he waited to report to the Second Mate, who was taking over the watch from Mr Patience. Underwood, when Patience had gone below, told Tom that if the wind should freshen further, there would be a need to shorten sail. 'I'll be glad of your assistance, and it'll be a good chance for you to learn,' he said.

They began walking the poop, back and forth, the Second Mate keeping a close eye on the canvas. Underwood was a friendly man of twenty-four, not long out of his apprenticeship but with the look of a good seaman about him. He drew Tom out, getting him to talk about his home and his reasons for coming to sea. Himself, he appeared to regard the sea as a fool's life.

'I made a mistake,' he said, 'and now I've to pay for it for the rest of my life. If you change your mind, change it quick—before it's too late.'

'I don't think I'll do that, sir.'

Underwood laughed. 'Don't be too sure. You've not seen anything yet.' He paused. 'The trouble comes when you want to settle down and make a home...get married. I left a girl behind in Liverpool—and that's where the rub is.' He added, 'Up to two years away, a week or two at home, then off again. You might just as well not bother, but there always comes the time when you want nothing more than to wed. And it's hard to leave the sea, believe me.'

'Why's that, sir?'

'Isn't it obvious? Who wants a seaman, ashore? What's the use of a man whose only qualification is that he can command a ship—can you tell me that?'

Tom, of course, could not; and paid little attention to what he saw as the softness of the Second Mate. The thought of marriage was so remote to Tom that he could afford to disregard the notion. After a while he continued his walk alone, buffeted by the wind, spattered now and again by flung spray, as Underwood moved right aft, keeping an eye on the sails and at intervals checking the course, looking over the helmsman's shoulder into the brightly polished brass binnacle. Underwood, intent upon the safety of the ship and the need to choose the right moment to call the Captain should Landon's presence on deck be necessary, failed to notice the shadowy figure of a man dodging along the deck towards the lifeboat.

Tom, however, was close to the break of the poop.

From the man's build and because of that afternoon's discovery Tom believed it to be the bosun. There was furtiveness in O'Connor's movements and Tom was certain now that he was up to no good. He wondered if he should draw Underwood's attention to the man now. But the given promise inhibited him. Besides, furtive or not, the bosun could be doing no more than his duty, intending as he had said to bring out the stowaway with the minimum fuss and danger. The situation to which Tom had given his agreement earlier had not altered: O'Connor had said he would deal with the matter at night when there were not so many men around to get hurt.

A moment later Tom saw the figure move suddenly, leaping up onto the lifeboat's tarpaulin cover. Then he saw the man's hand rise and fall, again and again, coming down in swift, smashing blows, possibly from a belaying-pin.

Murder was being attempted before his eyes.

# CHAPTER 6

Tom ran aft and unceremoniously grabbed the Second Mate's arm. 'It's the bosun, sir! On the lifeboat...hitting at something in the boat. Hitting at someone.'

Underwood ran to the break of the poop. 'What's going on?' he called.

There was no answer. Underwood called again: 'Is that you, O'Connor?'

After a pause there was a grudging response in a thick voice. 'Aye, it is.'

'What are you doing?'

'I thought I'd seen a movement beneath the lifeboat cover, and I suspected a stowaway.'

Underwood swore into the night. 'If you thought that, why did you not report to me first? What were you trying to do—kill him?'

'I was not!' O'Connor shouted back. 'What do you take me for, Mr Underwood? I was just trying to discourage him from showing fight when the cover came off, and that's all, so help me God!'

'You're very sure it's a stowaway, O'Connor.' With Tom behind him, the Second Mate slid fast down the poop ladder. Tom's mind was in a whirl; as he approached the lifeboat he saw the bosun's heavy face above him, saw the working of the lips, the almost animal snarl that was baring the man's teeth. There was a strong smell of drink, which could explain much. Tom stood by uncertainly as Underwood pulled himself up onto the skid and began loosing the canvas cover. The bosun was assisting him now, pulling the rope through the eyelets and then drawing back the tarpaulin, keeping the belaying-pin ready in one hand. At first nothing happened; then suddenly the bosun shouted, 'Watch out,' and lunged downward with the belaying-pin.

Tom found his voice. He called, 'Sir, look out, he has a pistol!'

Underwood had laid hold of the bosun's arm as a cry of pain came from inside the lifeboat. He twisted O'Connor's wrist savagely until the bosun let the weapon go. From the bottom of the boat a head emerged, and then a hand reached out and grasped the gunwale. There was a gash in the arm, and blood was running.

A face, thin and dark, stared around and then before anyone had reacted the man brought out his other hand in a sudden throwing motion and something went over the side into the sea.

Underwood asked, 'Did somebody say something about a pistol?'

'I did, sir—'

'Looks as if you may have been right. You too, O'Connor, in suspecting a stowaway, I'll say that much. There was still no need to behave as you did.' His voice was cutting as he went on, 'Or is a man's life not important to you?'

'Lives are cheap enough, mister, and well you know it,' the bosun answered roughly. 'What's one more or less?' He was breathing deeply, his chest heaving beneath his oilskin. The smell of drink was stronger than ever. 'Come out, you.' He grasped the arm of the stowaway and forced the hand free of the lifeboat's gunwale. 'Quick, now.'

The man rose in the boat and put a leg over the side. The Second Mate, jumping to the deck, gave him a hand down and then turned to Tom. 'That pistol. Did you see it? I mean, before he threw it?'

'Yes, sir.'

'Bosun?'

With heavy sarcasm O'Connor answered, 'The boy's right. I believed the stowaway had a pistol—which was why I was taking the precaution of a little work with the belaying-pin.'

Underwood nodded. 'There's a lot more explaining to be done yet, though.' He turned back to the stowaway, whom he was still holding, and thrust him against the bulwarks. 'Now: who are you, and what's your story?'

The man shrugged but didn't answer; in a patch of moonlight that broke just then through the cloud cover, Tom saw the watchful look in the eyes, saw the tight, scared face, the sallow-looking skin. The man, at a guess aged around thirty, was handsome and well-set-up and had no look of a villain. Underwood stared at him for a few moments and then said, 'All right. It'll keep a little longer, but I promise you you'll talk in the end.' He swung round on the bosun. 'What's *your* story, O'Connor?'

'My story, indeed? What about this—'

Underwood cut in sharply. 'I said, your story. Let's have it, man! How did you and young Chatto know the man had a pistol?'

O'Connor shrugged and said, 'Why, it was a guess, nothing more. I've had a few years' experience aboard windjammers, mister, more than the likes of you. If—'

'You said you saw it.'

'I never said that. It was the boy. Not me. I said I believed he had a pistol, that was all.'

Tom said, 'That's right, sir.'

'Then perhaps you'd care to explain instead, Chatto?'

Tom swallowed and looked appealingly at the bosun. He was out of his depth: a promise had been given. At home in the deanery promises had never been given lightly and, once given, had never been broken. It was a basic element of Tom's code. Now, it appeared likely to come into headlong collision with his duty, and aboard a ship duty would have to be put first. It was, in fact, the bosun who came to the aid of his conscience. Harshly he said, 'Leave the lad be. It wasn't his doing, mister. He found the man and he saw the pistol. He told me. I didn't want bloodshed aboard, so—'

'So you took the law into your own

hands and said nothing?'

'It was the better way,' the bosun said sullenly. 'I knew I could deal with it in my own time.'

'When in drink, and under cover of darkness, with few men around to see? I think I have your reasons, O'Connor, and you'll explain them yourself to the Captain during the forenoon. In the meantime, take the man to the fore peak—see he's securely locked in. First, see to it he's fed and watered—'

'There'll be no need for that, mister. I've already seen, he's made short work of the lifeboat's water and hard tack—and if there's anything dirtier than that aboard a ship at sea when the crew might need to man the boat, then I've—'

'I take the point, O'Connor, but what else would you expect a stowaway to do? In any case, he's to be provided with fresh water and stew from the galley. Then you'll replenish the lifeboat.' Underwood paused. 'One more thing: no rough stuff. He's to be properly treated or there'll be trouble. All right?'

'If you say so.'

'I say so.'

Scowling, the bosun seized the stowaway

by the shoulders and marched him off along the sloping deck towards the fo'c'sle. Underwood watched for a moment, then turned and climbed back to the poop. Tom followed. The Second Mate took a long look at the trim of the sails, then checked the compass. Satisfied, he put a hand on Tom's shoulder and led him across the poop, out of earshot of the man at the wheel. 'Better tell me the whole thing, Chatto. The Old Man's going to have to know in the morning. I may be able to help. It's plain O'Connor's been putting one over on you...there's nothing to be gained by holding back now.'

Tom told the Second Mate what had happened. Underwood didn't appear surprised. 'Pretty well as I thought. O'Connor meant to do that bloke in, rather than face what Mr Patience would have had to say when it was discovered O'Connor had neglected his duty. You see it, don't you?'

'I don't think I do,' Tom said, puzzled.

Underwood gave a quiet, humourless laugh. 'Oh, you'll learn! The sea's not a country parsonage, Chatto. It's the hell of a hard life. Maybe this gives some point to what I was telling you earlier. However hard the bloody life is, it's a damn sight harder ashore if no one wants you. Also, it's hard to step down from bosun to ordinary deckhand again, and that was on the cards, for there was trouble with Mr Patience last voyage too. O'Connor fancied that a corpse overboard was a better risk than a bad discharge for not having checked the lifeboat immediately before sailing.'

Next morning, Mr Patience came out from the saloon looking murderous himself: a First Mate was not paid to delegate everything to the bosun and Captain Landon had reminded him sharply of his own responsibilities. Patience was now looking for someone to hound for his life; and after his turn in the saloon came the bosun's and then Tom Chatto's. Tom found Captain Landon sitting alone by his fire, like a patriarch, one hand pulling at his thick, full beard. The eyes, startlingly blue, were not angry but grave, almost sad. The Old Man said quietly, 'I have the facts, boy. I shall give them to you, so that you may have the opportunity of disputing them if you wish.'

He did so. Then he asked, 'Well, boy?

Is there anything you disagree with?'

Tom shook his head. 'No, sir.'

There was an approving nod; on a bulkhead a brass-bound clock ticked away. It sounded abnormally loud to Tom in his tense frame of mind, ticking in time with the thump of his heart as he faced the lion-like figure by the fireplace. Landon said, 'I believe you're well enough aware of your own failing, boy, so I'll not stress it, except to say this.' He gave a deep, rumbling cough. 'Young you are, but not young enough to behave in a totally irresponsible way. It should have been as clear as day what the bosun was attempting to get away with, and you should have had more sense—aye, and more guts too, than to agree. Your duty was plain. Do I need to tell you that aboard a ship every man's duty is of over-riding importance in its observance, and that nothing else matters?'

'But a promise, sir?' Tom ventured.

The Old Man's eyebrows, white and heavy, went up but a more kindly look came over his face. 'A promise,' he said, 'obtained under threat.' He paused for a moment then went on, 'A promise is a promise and I'll never deny it. And I hold any man's personal honour as high as I hold my own. But you miss the point, which is that the promise should never have been given. To refuse to give it...that would have needed guts...and I think you have courage somewhere, Chatto. It's in your face. You have character. Use it, boy, use it.'

'Yes, sir.'

'Then remember it, and I'll say no more. There will be no punishment. I think you have suffered since yesterday.' Landon rose to his feet and wagged a finger in Tom's face. 'But if anything of this nature should occur again, you'll go to the mizzen fife-rail and a report may be made to the Line. Away with you, now.'

Tom left the saloon. In the half-deck that morning he asked Jim Wales what was meant by 'going to the mizzen fife-rail'. Wales told him: he'd be triced up at the rail through all kinds of weather until the Old Man ordered him to be cut down. 'It's done often enough, either the fife-rail or the rigging. Or the foretop. If you ask me, you've been damned lucky not to be sent there this time.' Then Wales lowered his voice. 'I'll tell you one thing, though, which I doubt if the Old Man himself would have thought fit to air officially. It's this: from now on, keep an eye lifting on O'Connor.'

That afternoon, while working with the hands on deck, Tom had a very nasty thought: had the bosun got away with his scheme, he, Tom Chatto, would have been an accessory to murder. He felt the blood drain from his face. It had been a narrow escape. It was an equally dispiriting thought that he was shipmates with a man who had been ready to commit murder for his own selfish ends, but this was something no one else had appeared to be concerned about in the least.

Tom felt that he was learning quite fast. And felt, too, that in the case of a future officer Mr Ralph's 'jodurecom' came into it somewhere.

During that same forenoon the stowaway had been interrogated by Landon and the First Mate. Very little had emerged beyond the fact that he was a Frenchman, and a sailor. He had been in the French Navy as a seaman gunner and when discharged on the expiry of his enlistment had gone to sea again, this time in a merchant vessel, still under the tricolour. His ship, the full-rigged *Aveyron,* had been unloading wines in Dublin when he had deserted. He had managed to cross to Liverpool as a stowaway in the steam packet out of Dublin, and had then stowed away again aboard the *Pass of Drumochter.*

'Why did you desert?' Landon asked, but the Frenchman wouldn't reply. His English was quite good enough to understand questioning but when Landon asked him twice more he still wouldn't give an answer.

Patience said, 'I'll get him talking sir.'

Landon looked quizzically at his First Mate. 'By the sound of it, Mr Patience, you mean to try short methods.'

'It's the only way, sir.'

'I take leave to doubt it. However...' The Old Man moved across the saloon to a porthole, where he looked out thoughtfully at the water, tumbling and rushing past below. Then he glanced at the compass, hanging in gimbals from the deckhead for the Master's personal check on the course. 'Very well, Mr Patience,' he said at last. 'Do what you can, but there is to be no cruelty. I intend,' he added, 'to work him with the hands, and I—'

'You're taking him on to Recife, are you?'

Landon raised his eyebrows. 'What else, Mr Patience?'

'We're not all that far out from England, sir.'

'Far enough, Mr Patience, far enough.'

The Mate shrugged; to return would cost the Line money in time lost, it was true. He went to the for'ard door of the saloon, telling the Frenchman, who had given his name as Paul Chardonnet, to go out ahead of him. When both men had left the saloon Landon went slowly back to the port and looked out at the sea for some minutes, frowning. He was still there when the door from the cabin opened behind him, then closed softly. Landon looked round, at first impatiently, then with a strangely gentle smile.

'Mary,' he said. 'It's all right, you may come in. Patience has gone about his work.'

She smiled. 'I know. Mr Patience has a loud voice. Do you really mean to carry the stowaway on to Recife, Theodore?'

'Certainly I do.'

Landon watched his wife as she sat in one of the leather-upholstered settees and laid her work bag beside her. As always when he looked at Mary he was struck by a sense of wonder that she had become his wife. Thirty years younger than he, she was fair and delicate, almost fragile. Beside her Landon felt boorish and uncouth on account of his size, on account of his sea-hardened hands that must surely, on occasion, be an affront to smooth white skin. Landon was a man of great physical strength still, a man of strong sensual appetite and, moreover, one who had married for the first time late in life. Often enough he was puzzled by Mary, as indeed he was puzzled, and always had been, by all women. There was an occasional abandonment in her response to him, an eagerness that sometimes he felt reached beyond the climax; and then after this there would be a curious frigidity and for many days thereafter he would feel inhibited from making any demands upon her.

He had been surprised, after their marriage some ten years before, how well she had taken to the sea life and the restricted living quarters afloat which were a poor substitute for a home ashore, or indeed for the ample house where she had

lived with her father in Manchester. Old
William Grimsdyke—no older in fact than
Theodore Landon—had been a middling
prosperous merchant in the town; when,
a widower, he had re-married. Mary had
not wished to remain on in the house with
her stepmother. Landon often wondered
how much that fact had had to do with
her acceptance of his proposal—not, most
certainly, that she had ever given him cause
to ponder on that; it was a mere passing if
recurrent thought and was due to Landon's
need to find some rational explanation of
why so attractive a girl should have wished
to marry a man of her father's age and, as
a natural consequence, change her way of
life so drastically.

Looking up from her sewing Mary asked,
'Will you be able to, Theodore?'

'What, my dear? Able to do what?'

'Why, land the man at Recife.' She bit
off an end of cotton with small white
teeth.

'Why not? There's a British consul in
Recife. The matter should be easily enough
settled.'

'He'll need to be repatriated, Theodore.
I'm thinking of the expense to the Line.
What will Mr John have to say?'

Landon shrugged his heavy shoulders irritably. 'Why, he'll understand the situation, you may be sure.'

'I'm not so sure. He may blame the Master who put him to such expense.'

'He may,' Landon answered shortly. 'That will have to be accepted if necessary.'

She sighed. 'I do wish this hadn't happened, Theodore. Could you not change your mind, and put back to an English port such as Falmouth, or perhaps Cork?'

'No,' Landon said forcefully. 'I can't do that. The loss of revenue involved in such a delay would be far greater than the expense of a stowaway's passage home—far greater. Mary, you're making a mountain out of a molehill—in a case like this the Board's not going to worry about a few wretched sovereigns!'

'Very well, Theodore, it's your decision, of course...but as for me, I'd feel happier if that man were put ashore as soon as possible.' She looked at her husband, a level, direct gaze from large brown eyes—lovely eyes, Landon thought with a sudden hunger, in a very lovely face. 'Call it a silly woman's fears if you will, dearest, but I believe he'll bring us trouble.

Besides which,' she added on a suddenly crisp note, 'I don't like the French and never will.'

Landon smiled, moved towards her, bent and took her head gently in his big hands. 'And there we have it,' he said. 'No more than prejudice, just like a woman.' He kissed her, then stood up. 'You must stop worrying. Patience will have him well in hand and will find out all about him. By the way, you might take a look at his arm, my dear, when Patience has done with him. It needs washing and bandaging, I think.'

Patience was doing his best. Before locking the Frenchman in the fore peak he had taken him to the galley for questioning, ordering Joshua Leggatt to leave them. Once alone Patience had lost no time. 'Let's have it, Chardonnet. And the truth, mind.'

'I say nothing.'

'You don't like speaking the truth, is that it? Come on now, Frenchy: why did you desert your ship?'

'I say nothing.'

It was no use; each time, each question, the answer was the same. Patience grew angry. He disregarded Landon's injunction against force. He reached out and gave the Frenchman two hard, stinging slaps across the face. 'Come along, you Frog bastard! Out with it or begod you'll suffer!'

Chardonnet glared back at the Mate furiously; his eyes were red-rimmed from sheer tiredness and hunger, but when he suddenly clenched his fists and took a step forward, Patience chose to regard the look in those eyes as that of a madman and reacted accordingly. Taking a step back himself, the Mate's rump made painful contact with the edge of Joshua Leggatt's iron stove. He roared out an oath. The Frenchman made the mistake of laughing and Patience saw red.

Lunging forward, he thrust Chardonnet hard back against the bulkhead, lashed out in a heavy blow to the man's face, nimbly dodged the return one, and then, with one hairy arm keeping Chardonnet pinned back, reached behind him until he contacted the handle of a vast iron pot containing a simmering stew for the crew's dinner.

He dragged at it. The Frenchman gave a high yell. It was Leggatt who averted a nasty situation just in time. Hearing the cry he dashed back into the galley, seized a thick cloth and bore down with it on the lid of the pot, pinning it to the stove with all his strength.

'Oh no you don't, mister!' he shouted.

'Get out of my way, you—'

Leggatt shook his head. 'That pot stays right where it is, mister. I don't 'old no brief for the bloody Frenchy, but if I was you I'd not want to swing for the likes of 'im.'

Slowly, his face mottled and congested, the Mate subsided. Still breathing heavily, he removed his hand from the pot's handle but kept the flat of a palm hard against the Frenchman's chest. His voice thick with fury he said, 'There'll be other ways, you damn French bastard. I'll ask you again: *why did you desert your ship?*'

The Frenchman grinned. 'So. I will tell. I desert because the Mate of the ship, he also was a one damn big bastard bully.'

He met Patience's eye. Patience seemed to swell visibly, but with Leggatt present he decided upon discretion. He was certain the Frenchman's given reason was not the true one but he didn't propose to lose further dignity by going on with a probably hopeless inquisition.

He said, 'Out, Frenchy. Go for'ard. We'll see what a spell in the fore peak does for your tongue.'

Joshua Leggatt gave a wide grin when the two had turned away. Out on deck, Tom Chatto, engaged under the Second Mate on overhauling the seizings around the stay thimbles in preparation for heavier weather ahead, watched the two men going along by the bulwarks, and noted their expressions. The sooner they made Recife, the better it would be.

Throughout that day Captain Landon was to be seen continually studying the barometer and watching the slow fall in pressure that warned of the heavy weather on their track that his trained eye had seen already in the cloud formation. He felt in his bones that he was sailing into weather worse than normal for the area and the time of year; and, good seaman that he was, he acted at once upon his instinct.

The order was passed for All Hands.

The watch below turned out to join those on deck, grumbling, to prepare the *Pass of Drumochter* for what might be an ordeal. Below decks everything movable was doubly secured against the heave of wind and water. On the deck itself all lashings were examined carefully and where necessary double-banked. Mr Patience along with the bosun opened up the tween-deck hatches and carried out such inspection of the cargo and the shifting-boards as was possible. Aloft, the gear was overhauled for good measure—the footropes, the ratlines and shrouds, one or two new buntlines and leechlines were rove—real sailorman's work in which the apprentices assisted. So did the Frenchman, who had been released from the fore peak by Landon's order and had had his arm bandaged by Mrs Landon. He was walking, as it happened, close to Tom Chatto, who noticed how deft the stowaway was, and how conscientiously he worked. At one moment Chardonnet caught Tom's eye and grinned cheerfully. Above the rising wind he shouted, 'You are surprised, perhaps, is this not so—surprised that I work for a ship that is not my own, and for a bastard of a Mate?'

Tom grinned back but didn't answer. Chardonnet went on, 'I work for the old *Capitaine*. A good old man, that one.' Then he grinned again, and rolled his eyes, and made a curious gesture with his fingers, forming a circle with thumb and forefinger. 'Or perhaps for the *madame,* who can tell?'

Tom looked at him dubiously but Chardonnet had already turned his back. From his position on the main yard Tom looked down on the work proceeding on deck: all skylights were being battened down and secured with tarpaulins, all inessential deckhouse doors were being caulked up to prevent any inrush of water if they should ship a heavy sea or two in the hours ahead. Men were standing by the halliards and braces as Landon, from the poop, ordered the royal yards to be sent down and the flying jib unbent. Landon, Tom saw, was watching the sails closely, and kept speaking to the man at the wheel, occasionally lending a hand himself to bring the ship quickly to the shifts of the wind, which was now beginning to become oddly erratic.

At last, after what had seemed endless hours of hard and exhausting labour, Landon conferred with Mr Patience and Underwood, cast a long look aloft, walked along the upper deck for another careful scrutiny, and then pronounced the ship as ready and secure as men could make her.

'Send the port watch below,' he ordered. 'And hot cocoa for all hands, if you please, Mr Patience.'

Tom was grateful for the cocoa which Leggatt sloshed into his tin mug. He took it along to the half-deck and found Horatio Mainprice sitting on a lower bunk looking white and tired. Coming along the deck, Tom had noticed a drop in the wind and he remarked on this. Mainprice said, 'I know. That's a bad sign. The calm before the storm. Didn't you realize?'

'No, I didn't. Who told you—Vice-Admiral Sir Thingummy Bilgekeel?'

Mainprice didn't appear to register the sacrilege. With full seriousness he said, 'I just feel it, that's all. Don't you?'

Tom gave a short laugh. 'I can't say I do, nipper.'

'You will before much longer.' Mainprice looked suddenly irritated. 'For heaven's sake, Chatto, don't *you* call me nipper. We're practically the same age, damn it.' He added, 'I don't like the bloody word anyway. It's childish. They wouldn't call anyone that aboard a warship.'

'I believe,' Tom said maliciously, memory bringing back a book he'd once read, 'they call them warts.' He didn't get any response to that for the door had opened. Jim Wales came in, leaving the door ajar; looking through Tom could see the Atlantic in the fading light, flat but with an oily swell and somehow threatening, like a bottomless, evil pool. The wind seemed to have gone altogether now; Tom could hear the *slat-slat* sound as limp canvas flopped back against masts and yards, and the rattle of the blocks as they hung loose. There was something vaguely unnerving about it.

Wales looked at the two apprentices. 'Out on deck,' he said briefly. 'It's to be All Hands again in a brace of shakes.'

'What's going on now?' Horatio asked.

Wales, too, looked tired and strained. 'The Old Man's ordered the storm mains'l to be sent to the main yard. That means he expects a real blow. It won't be just playing about, not tonight. You'd best remember the golden rule aboard windjammers: one hand for the ship—and one for yourselves!'

He went out on deck. Tom and Horatio came out behind him and were seized upon by Mr Patience and sent to join the hands of the watch coming along the deck to begin unbending the ordinary mainsail. Swarming up the shrouds to the main yard, Tom looked aft towards the poop. The Captain was there still, and now Mrs Landon was with him; they were talking together, though the Old Man was keeping his eye on the sails and the likely direction from which the wind, when it came, would strike. The sea still had that flat and oily look, and now the last of the daylight was beginning to go. Ahead on the starboard bow a long low line of black cloud had formed, and above it, the colour seeming to arise from out of it, the sky was green-shot and dangerous-looking. As Tom looked towards this great bank of cloud he saw a curious transformation of the sea's surface, a sort of ruffling movement that spread from ahead with extreme rapidity and came down towards the ship.

There was a shout from the poop. *'All hands! All hands on deck!* Mr Patience, we have the wind, west-nor'westerly. Take in—'

Very suddenly, Landon's voice broke off. Something seemed to have gone badly wrong on the poop; the spanker boom had swung wildly across the deck, heavy and fast, lethal to anything in its way. Men were shouting, and when the boom went smartly back the other way Tom could see no sign of Mary Landon—until something in the water, no more than a break of spray in the near darkness, caught his eye and he saw the white face staring up. A moment later there was a cry from aloft, from the main topgallant-mast, and a figure, turning from the shrouds, was seen to be diving into the sea.

Somebody—Tom fancied it was Horatio Mainprice—shouted above the whine of the rising gale, *'It's the Frenchie!'*

## CHAPTER 7

Patience called away the lifeboat: he had taken charge on the instant. The swell was now breaking into long waves with spray coming from their tops as the wind struck with vicious suddenness. A lifebuoy spun from the after lee rail, down towards Mary Landon and the man who could now be seen fighting through the water.

Patience ran to the skids and lent a hand himself with launching the lifeboat; already the chain gripes had been freed. On the poop the Second Mate and two hands had got a line over the arm of the spanker boom—it had parted its three-and-a-half-inch hemp guy pendant—and the wild swing was under control. Before the lifeboat had begun to move on the skids Captain Landon saw what the First Mate intended. He called out, 'Avast there—secure the lifeboat! Mr Patience, come aft at once and we'll get a line over.'

'That's not the way—'

'At once, Mr Patience! You will obey my order at once.'

His face furious, the First Mate went aft. Landon had already thrown a line, but the wind had taken it well away. That wind was gusting strongly, hitting the ship with blows from the darkness like the fists of a giant, laying her over hard to leeward. The two faces in the water could scarcely be seen now. Landon was passing the order to back the topsails to take the way off the ship; the royals and topgallants were already off her. Even so, and even though hardly a minute had passed since Mary Landon had gone overboard, the ship was drawing ahead. There was no time for argument and Patience, grabbing for a hand line, gathered it into his hands and sent it spinning expertly towards the lifebuoy which Mary and the Frenchman were now clinging onto.

The monkey's-fist at the end of the line took the water close. Chardonnet reached out and grasped it; the Frenchman had his other arm around Mary Landon. The Mate heaved in on the line, assisted by Landon and Underwood. Within another couple of minutes the lifebuoy had been drawn to the ship's side. A heavier line was sent down fast, and skilfully the Frenchman put a bowline around Mary Landon. They were hauled up the ship's side and assisted, gasping, over the lee bulwarks. Landon took his wife in his arms, wordlessly, for a moment; then released her as the steward came up to take her below. He seized the Frenchman's hand and shook it warmly. 'That was a brave action,' he said. 'Thank you—from the bottom of my heart. I shall not forget, you may be sure.'

Chardonnet made a gesture of negation and turned away, going back to his work. Landon caught the Mate's eye. 'Look at the weather,' he said. 'No man could expect to send away a lifeboat tonight, Mr Patience, as you should well know.'

Within three minutes the ship had been struck by a wind of near-hurricane force.

Tom had been sent for'ard to assist in getting the headsails off; the jibs and foretopmast stays'ls had been sent down. But by this time a good deal of damage had been done already; the fore and main upper topsails had been blown clear from the boltropes, whipped away into the night. On the fo'c'sle Tom Chatto, battered by a screaming wind, his head in a whirl, wondered how the crew could possibly identify any rope in that spider's-web of sheets, braces lifts and stays as the spindrift flew into their faces from the wave-tops and the solid water swept the decks to knock the feet from under their straining bodies. Tom himself had had a tough job to reach the fo'c'sle at all; the ship was taking it green and heavy over the weather rails and was riding sluggishly, wallowing, the washports about as much use as a punt's baler against the constant inrush. He'd struggled along waist-deep in swirling water that forced the breath from his lungs and half drowned him as he went right under, hanging onto the lifelines and waiting for the seas to drain away from above his head as half the Atlantic Ocean, so it seemed, pounded aboard and fought to subdue the ship.

Over all, and alarming to a first-voyager, was an infernal din, a ghastly and horrifying shriek of wind in fury. And just before Tom reached the fo'c'sle-head the forecourse joined the upper topsails, ripping out from the cringles, hanging for a moment from the rovings and then whipping away out of sight with a crack that sounded clear above the gale. Patience was laying about himself like a lunatic when Tom reached him, driving the hands on to get the remaining headsails off in accordance with Landon's order. Toil and sweat and breaking muscles did it—that, and time. It seemed to Tom that they had been all night taking in the fore lower topsail alone by the time they had clewed it up to windward, with the sail itself full of wind, and lowered away the halliards and eased off the lee sheet, clewed the yard down and then hauled up on the lee clewline and the buntlines—all in that screaming wind and the darkness with the ship laid over to such an extent that the men on the footropes had been swept viciously through an arc of some seventy degrees as they fought to keep their footholds. Even when that job was done the ship didn't seem to have been eased much. She lurched and laboured still, the topgallant and royal masts bending and whipping under the strain.

Tom heard the shout from aft: 'Clew up for reefing, main lower tops'l...let go mains'l halliards!'

Sweating next to Tom was Jim Wales. He said, 'Looks as if the Old Man means to ride it out under no more than lowered tops'ls, close reefed.'

Dimly through the murk Tom saw a figure leave the poop—the Second Mate, he fancied—while others went to the halliards belayed to the pinrail. Underwood leapt above the rushing waters into the shrouds, racing his men to the main lower topsail yard to take his place at the weather earring for the reefing operation. Underwood was aloft quickly, seeing the yard well down in the lifts and then laying out to the weather yardarm; by the time his men were on the yard he had his earring rove. He hauled it taut and made it fast and when the job was done in the teeth of the still-increasing wind, he shifted to take the bunt for furling the main course.

Just after he'd done so there was a

tremendous lurch that threw Tom off his feet. He went sprawling, sliding for the side. Patience caught him just in time, grabbing him by the scruff of the neck. By now the wind had come almost abeam and they were not getting the sails off quickly enough. Another heavy gust struck, pressing relentlessly against the vessel, forcing her over and over until the lower yardarms on the lee side seemed scarcely to clear the water that surged up to them; the yards seemed to Tom to form an up-and-down, almost vertical link between the sea and the sky.

The Mate gave a gasp of relief when, slowly, the ship came upright again. It had been a near thing: they had been in danger of being put over onto their beam-ends. But when the canvas was at last off her and she was down to close-reefed lower topsails, she rode easier and the hands were set to work on clearing up the tangle left behind. This done, the word was passed for one watch to go below. They went with soaked clothing to their straw palliases in the fo'c'sle accommodation where some four inches of dirty water sloshed the deck. It was no better in the half-deck, as Tom found. He turned in wet and shivering and lay there in his narrow bunk listening to the sounds of the storm and the thump and rattle of the blocks.

Roused out again soon after dawn for his watch on deck, he went out into cold greyness and close horizons, with the wind still howling through the rigging and the spray still being flung along the deck. There was, however, not so much solid water coming over now. When during the afternoon watch the wind lessened considerably the hands were set to work bending new canvas in place of the lost sails and in renewing ropes and once again overhauling as much of the other gear as could be attended to in the prevailing weather.

Tom asked the senior apprentice why all this overhauling hadn't been done before sailing. Wales laughed and said, 'It's partly a question of time, but it's mainly money. Even Porter Holt watch the pennies these days. They don't give us enough shore riggers and they don't authorize much expenditure anyway, not unless some gear breaks or the ropes are so worn they just have to be replaced. That apart...why, it's left to the wind and sea to show 'em up.'

'Couldn't that lead to men being lost?'

'Oh,' Wales said carelessly, 'lives are cheap enough.' And he added, 'You'll learn.'

One thing Tom had learned during that night of storm was that when the ship was threatened all the men worked together remarkably well, old scores and jealousies forgotten while the danger lasted. Even the drunk who'd been laid into by the bosun just before sailing worked with a will to O'Connor's orders. And as for the stowaway, Paul Chardonnet was a hero now. The Old Man's wife was much liked aboard, as was Landon himself. Later that day the weather settled into much easier conditions under a dead grey sky with a heaving deep-sea swell left behind by the gale, and Chardonnet was bidden to the saloon. He was there for some fifteen minutes and when he came out Tom heard the Mate speaking to him.

'Get a kiss of gratitude, did you?' the Mate asked sardonically.

'I am sure you would like to know, m'sieur.' Chardonnet added, 'M'sieu' le capitaine, he give me a glass of rum.'

'I can smell that for myself,' Patience said. 'Well, you did a brave thing and that

134

I'll not deny. But don't let it go to your head. No favours. You'll work as hard as anyone else aboard.' Patience moved away. The Frenchman, going along the deck with a cocksure swagger, caught Tom's eye.

'A driver of men, that,' he said. 'Him I do not like. Him I would kill most willingly.' Then, suddenly, he looked alarmed, as if regretting an indiscretion. 'I ask you not to tell this,' he said, then went off for'ard, swaggering again along the slippery deck. Tom looked after him, frowning; a man didn't have to be treated as a criminal, surely, for deserting a ship aboard which he'd been driven past the point where he could take no further bullying. Chardonnet seemed a decent man and there had been no thought of self when he had dived into the sea from aloft. Tom had heard from Uncle Benjamin that there was more vicious bullying aboard foreign ships than would be tolerated aboard vessels under the British flag.

Next day there was an accident whilst the hands were aloft shaking out the topgallantsails on the fore and main masts.

A young seaman named Ballantyne, one of the more clumsy ones, lost his footing on the fore topgallant yard and went crashing. In his fall he hit a man on the upper topsail yard and this man also lost his balance. The first man went into the water on the flat of his back, the second came down hard on the bulwarks, gave a shriek of agony and collapsed inboard. Men ran to pick him up whilst, this time, Patience was allowed to send away the lifeboat to search for Ballantyne, who had disappeared.

The lifeboat's crew failed to find him during an hour's search, after which time Landon, with a heavy heart, ordered the boat back for hoisting. In the meantime the second man, an elderly Irishman named Lacey, had died: his back was broken and his end, tended in the saloon by Mary Landon, had been a painful one. Tom Chatto was shaken: he would never forget the look in old Lacey's eyes as he was picked up from the scuppers wet and cold and bleeding from superficial damage and obviously dying even then. As soon as the Captain had pronounced him dead the body was taken to the sailmaker to be sewn in canvas. Patience came to the half-deck and ordered the junior apprentices to cut along and watch.

'As officers—we hope—in due course, you'll need to have all the sea trades at your fingertips,' he said. 'This is but one of them. I'm no ghoul...it's my job to see to it that you are given every opportunity to learn.'

Tom, with Mainprice and Allan, went to where the sailmaker was sitting on deck by the corpse. They watched as the canvas shroud was cut and fitted, as the sailmaker threaded his needle and, with the assistance of a hard leather shield known as a 'palm', started sewing. The last stitch was driven through the nose of the corpse. Tom gave an involuntary gasp.

'Feeling squeamish, boy?' the sailmaker asked with a grin. Like the dead man he was elderly, wizened and brown and small, with sharp blue eyes, a man, as befitted his trade, of deft hand movements. 'It'd never do,' he went on, 'to let a shipmate go over without the stitch through the nose. It wards off the evil spirits that would otherwise plague a decent-living sailorman.' He gave a grotesque cackle, his eyes vanishing in the mass of wrinkles.

For the remainder of the watch the body, weighted at the feet with pig-iron ballast, lay in its canvas shroud, under the break of the fo'c'sle, and at three bells in the twelve to four watch a plank was rigged to the bulwarks with the corpse upon it. Captain Landon came from the saloon to read a short service and old Lacey was slid from the tilted plank into the sea, from under the Red Ensign that he had served with his life; and afterwards the work of the ship went on as before.

## CHAPTER 8

Those sudden deaths had brought Tom hard up against the bleak fact that one slip of hand or foot, one moment's lack of care, could, aboard a sailing ship, put any man into one of the sailmaker's dreadful canvas shrouds. To Tom there had been indecency in the haste with which old Lacey had been dispatched overboard.

Not so, according to Jim Wales.

'Sailors are a superstitious bunch,' he said. 'A body aboard is bad luck.' There was a twinkle in his eye when he added, 'Almost as bad as a parson.'

'Is a parson bad luck?'

'A Holy Joe's the very worst sort of Jonah,' Wales said solemnly. But there was no Holy Joe aboard the *Pass of Drumochter;* and the body had gone. And with it the bad luck did seem, oddly, to have gone as well. The next forenoon there was a great improvement in the weather as the sun broke through, shining soon after from a clear blue sky as the clouds retreated towards the south-east. The ship bowled along with a fresh wind filling her sails; Landon was pressing on under all canvas to the royals. That day it was a pleasure to go aloft.

From the mainmast crosstrees Tom looked down on the poop, the scrubbed deck with the polished brass of the binnacle reflecting the sun in brilliant fire. Landon was pacing, stopping now and again to run a hand along the well-tended teakwood rails. After a while Mary Landon came up and they paced the deck arm in arm. Landon, considerate as ever, had taken over the watch from Mr Underwood, who was catching up on some sleep.

Tom contrasted the currently idyllic scene with the filthy weather and dangers of recent days. It had been a bad experience, but, once over, Tom was glad it had happened. Next time wouldn't seem so bad, and he had learned to keep steady, to keep his head at a time of stress. He was beginning to glory in being part of a man's world.

In the half-deck that evening Jim Wales said casually, 'It's a good thing we've got the Frenchie aboard as it's turned out.'

Tom nodded; already he was realizing that every man counted aboard a wind-jammer and to be short-handed was potentially dangerous. Wales went on, 'He's a good seaman, the Frenchy, one of the best. Pity he's got up against Patience. Our First Mate doesn't like Frenchies at the best of times, and this one's got right up his nose.'

'Because he wouldn't say why he'd deserted?'

'Largely, of course. Patience never did like being bested—who does? But there's an element of jealousy as well, I believe.'

Horatio Mainprice, butting in, asked, 'The Old Man's wife?' He gave a suggestive snigger.

'No need to sound lecherous about it,' Wales said coldly. 'It doesn't become you at your age, nipper—and it wasn't what I meant anyway.' He paused. 'Patience likes to be in her good books, that's all, and now he feels the Frenchy's stolen his thunder—which I'd say he has. Besides, Chardonnet's the sort women like.'

Mainprice began again. 'You mean—'

'I mean exactly what I said and no more.' Wales frowned down at his plate of cracker hash for a while then went on, 'God knows, sailors are a randy enough crowd as soon as they touch port—you'll see—and a windjammer isn't a very willing monastery. But they're a decent bunch basically, and Landon's liked. Many masters aren't but he is.'

'So Patience won't be poddle-faking around the saloon, forcing his attentions on the Old Man's lady wife before the Frenchy gets a foot in the door?' Mainprice laughed.

Jim Wales waved a fork at him. 'I don't like that sort of talk, nipper, and I won't have it in the half-deck. A word from me to the Mate and you'll do a spell in the hen-coop with the hens for company. Just bear it in mind, will you?'

'Sorry,' Horatio said, but was quite unabashed. 'Suppose she wants...that sort of thing? After all, the Old Man's years older—'

Wales got to his feet with a sudden movement, his face furious. Taking the apprentice by the lapels of his pea-jacket he hoisted him to his feet and thrust him back savagely against a bunk-board. 'You've got a filthy little mind for your age, haven't you? It's overdue to have its bilges cleaned out. You'll leave your tea and get out on deck and let the wind blow through it for a couple of hours. And when you come back, you'll tell me the name of every rope that's secured along the starboard side of the ship, taking 'em from for'ard to aft. If you get one wrong, you start all over again. All right?'

'I'm on watch at—'

'And don't you argue with me, nipper, or it'll be the worse for you for a long, long time to come. Out!' He heaved the protesting youth to the door and pushed him out. Then, banging the door shut again, he came back to where Tom was sitting. 'Filthy little scum,' he said, and gave a short laugh. 'Supercilious little bugger—not worth worrying about really, I s'pose, though where I come from...'

When Wales didn't go on Tom asked curiously, 'Where do you come from...if you don't mind my asking?'

'Of course I don't. Derbyshire. Small village over by Swanwick.'

'Isn't that a mining area?'

Wales nodded. 'My father was a miner. All his life. It killed him. Choked his lungs till he couldn't breathe. It's as hard a life as this. Soon after he died, my mother died as well...from consumption. It was the conditions, you see.' He gave another laugh, a hard one. 'Bloody coal owners...and shipowners are no better by and large. Starvation wages, skimped equipment, holding men's lives dirt cheap.' He shrugged. 'A man had to do what he must, though, and try not to grumble while he's doing it. My father...his father was down the mines before him, and with Dad it was a matter of pride to do the job well and not complain. Or try not to.'

'You didn't want to follow him?'

'At first, yes. I was that sort of a fool. I'm one of a family of ten, and my elder sister had the lot of us on her hands after our mum and dad died. She slaved herself to the bone to provide for us until some of us could earn to help out. Me, I've had no education to speak of, or none beyond what I've been able to glean by reading and study. I did work down the mines for two years as a kid, and I studied when I wasn't working, and then I left the mine and came to sea. My sister had saved the money to pay for an apprenticeship, you see, and it was her dream that I'd command a ship one of these days.'

'I wonder how she came to think of the sea?' Tom asked.

'It wasn't her, boyo, it was me, and she made it possible, and made her dream fit mine. I'd read a lot about the sea, and I'd been once to Liverpool and seen the big ships moving in and out, and I'd read a lot about the world and I wanted to see it. I'd have shipped in the fo'c'sle and tried to reach the afterguard that way, through the hawse pipe as we say. But Lorna would have none of that.' There was a touch of real pride in his voice. 'Not only that, but she sent me to Porter Holt rather than to some ill-found coasting company that take their apprentices and officers less choosily. I've a lot to be thankful for and I know it.'

He stopped there, abruptly, as if he felt he'd said too much. Tom was flattered that the senior apprentice should have opened his heart to him as far as he had; he felt a sense of *rapport* with Jim Wales, perhaps more than he'd ever felt with anyone else in his life, which was strange considering the vast difference between their two backgrounds. He also felt that Wales' confidences had been sparked off by what Horatio Mainprice had hinted about Mary Landon, and if this was the case then his regard for the Captain's wife was as high as it so obviously was for his sister Lorna.

The days passed; the oldest canvas was sent aloft for the tropics and for a while they lay in the Doldrums, that oppressive region of cloudless, torrid skies broken by occasional violent squalls, situated between the north-east and south-east trade winds. It was like being in a vapour bath, and the daily ritual of serving out the fresh water was more than usually looked forward to. Each day at eight bells in the afternoon throughout the voyage, the fresh-water pump was shipped and filled buckets were carried to the galley, the fo'c'sle, the half-deck and the Captain's pantry. After the Doldrums came the Equator, where Tom Chatto and Horatio Mainprice were duly ducked in accordance with seafaring custom.

Some four weeks after Tom's talk with Jim Wales, by which time favourable winds had brought the *Pass of Drumochter* in towards the South American coast and a day's sailing from Recife, Landon sent for Mr Patience to come to the saloon where he poured two small measures of whisky.

A toast was drunk, then Landon sat back, lifting his head to stare for a few moments at the deckhead. Then he said, 'Mr Patience...there is the matter of Chardonnet. What's your opinion of him?'

'A good seaman, sir.'

'That is my opinion also. I've watched him a great deal, both on deck and aloft. At the wheel I find him a capable helmsman, with a good eye and a sensitive touch, able to respond well to the ship. One finds too few such natural sailors today.'

'That's true,' the Mate said.

'Tomorrow we make Recife. We're one hand short, even with Chardonnet. I can't afford to lose him, Mr Patience.'

Patience sat forward, his face bleak. 'You don't mean to carry him on, surely? That's against all—'

'I'm in need of him, Mr Patience.'

'I've no doubt we can sign on more hands in Recife.'

'Yes, I agree. But what sort of hands? Better the devil we know...and devil would likely enough be the right word for what we might find in Recife!'

'But the British consul—'

'And Chardonnet knows the ship in bad weather, Mr Patience. With Cape Horn ahead that's important, you'll agree.'

'Aye,' the Mate said, sounding most disagreeable, 'but you'll remember we don't yet know the truth of why he deserted his last ship, and that's something I'd much welcome word of, before I work any longer with a Frenchman.'

Landon wagged a finger at him. 'You mustn't allow your personal prejudices to influence your judgment, Mr Patience. That is scarcely the way that leads to command.' There was a glint of wicked amusement in Landon's eye when he went on, 'In any case, Chardonnet has spoken of what he terms, if I remember, a bullying so-and-so of a First Mate. I do not for one moment condone desertion—but as God's my judge, Mr Patience, I've known mates who well fit that description and

I've known fine seamen desert because of them.' He sat back. 'No, Mr Patience, I shall take Chardonnet on with me after I've had words with the authorities in Recife.'

A few minutes later on the poop Patience let off steam to the Second Mate. 'I don't know why the old fossil ever bothered to ask my opinion at all,' he stormed. 'His mind was made up long before he ever opened his mouth.'

He stumped away for'ard. Paul Chardonnet happened to be in the waist, and Patience halted. 'I suppose you know,' he said harshly, 'what the Captain is proposing for you, Frenchy?'

Chardonnet nodded. 'Yes, *m'sieur*. He has asked if I am willing.'

'Are you?'

'Yes, *m'sieur*. I am happy aboard this ship.' Chardonnet went on with a face of pure innocence, 'A ship with such a kind gentleman for a Mate...you understand, no?'

Patience flushed. 'Don't you get funny with me,' he snarled. Restraining himself he marched away to the fo'c'sle-head, found Horatio Mainprice in his path and proceeded to make that young gentleman's life a misery for the next few minutes.

Patience was under no illusions as to how he was regarded by the crew, and Chardonnet in particular—yet the Frenchman was prepared to sail on with him. Patience was convinced that there was some other reason than a bullying mate for that desertion—and that the man did not wish to be landed in Recife. Patience intended to find out more before the *Pass of Drumochter* left the port behind her.

Next morning the ship came in towards the land under a clear blue sky. Tom, on watch with Patience, heard for the first time the welcome cry from the foretopgallant masthead: *'Land ho!'*

He was sent below to call the Captain. Coming on deck, Landon climbed into the mizzen shrouds and stared ahead through his telescope. It was not long before Tom made out the long, low coastline of Pernambuco, with a hint of high ground far behind. He felt a surge of excitement at his first sight of a foreign land as the *Pass of Drumochter* bowled along under a fair wind.

Some eight miles distant from the port Landon passed the word for all hands and had the canvas taken off, proceeding thence under reefed topsails alone and now flying the flag signal for a tug and pilot. Backing his topsails a little later he hove the ship to outside the entry to the channel and lay off to await the tug.

Patience stared towards the port from the weather rail. A few minutes later he drew Landon's attention to a column of smoke approaching from the direction of the town. 'That'll be the PSNC coming out for home, no doubt,' he said in reference to the regular steamship schedule of the Pacific Steam Navigation Company.

Landon's telescope went up again. 'She's a PSNC right enough but she's the *Orcoma* out of Liverpool for Valparaiso. She'll turn south for the Horn presently.' He shut his telescope with a smart blow of his palm. 'She'll have left Liverpool a long while after us, Mr Patience. There should be mail waiting.'

Tom overheard that remark with pleasure, though his father was a poor letter-writer and might not have written in time to catch a mail within a couple of weeks or so of his son's sailing: more likely he would be waiting to hear from Tom first.

Soon after Landon had spoken a tug was seen coming out. Landon took over on the poop, and Tom was sent for'ard with Patience to stand by for the tug's line. After the customary bargaining with the Master, the steam tug was made fast and the pilot, a scruffy little man in a singlet and importantly peaked cap, came aboard. Landon ordered the remainder of the canvas off and the *Pass of Drumochter* proceeded inwards under bare poles in the care of the chuffing tug with its filthy coal-smoke tarnishing the spotless decks of the sailing ship, to the fury of the Mate.

On arrival in the roads Landon was ordered by the port authority to anchor and await notification of a discharging berth. And there they swung incommunicado for two full days, during which tempers flared among the men, not least because the expected mail was not sent out. Several ships, British and foreign, passed them on their way seawards; and two more arrivals, sailing ships in ballast, were admitted ahead of the *Pass of Drumochter* to go alongside the loading berths. But, at last, the fresh tug and pilot came out for them, the anchor was brought home, the links of the cable were washed down with the salt-water hoses, and they went inwards for discharge.

While Patience got his hatch covers off and prepared to get up the cargo, which was a part cargo of cased machine parts, Captain Landon went ashore to see the British consul and the Porter Holt agent, leaving his wife aboard. After a while Tom Chatto, working about the upper deck with Mainprice and Allan under the bosun, saw Mrs Landon come up from the saloon companion carrying a basket and walk for'ard towards the fo'c'sle. Before reaching it she vanished down the companion just for'ard of Number One cargo hatch.

Patience had seen her as well. Frowning, he caught Tom's eye. He roared at him, 'You, boy. My compliments to Mrs Landon. Warn her to stay clear of the bosun's store. Tell her the bloody Frenchy's working down there...and if I had my way he'd be off the ship by now.'

Tom said, 'He'd never hurt Mrs Landon, sir!'

'Don't argue with me, boy, just do as I say and be quick about it or I'll have you tarring down the mainmast, so help me God if I don't.'

Tom nipped fast down the companion and saw the Captain's wife going down the next ladder, a vertical one leading to the bosun's store. He called the warning as ordered by the Mate.

Mary Landon looked up. 'I know,' she said in her light, clear voice. 'Thank you, Tom—but tell Mr Patience he really needn't worry about me.'

Tom hesitated. 'Yes, but ma'am—'

'Go on, Tom. Do as I say—please.' She looked up at him, and smiled. Below, Tom could see Chardonnet's face, also smiling. Tom, realizing suddenly that the Captain's lady was stationary on a vertical ladder with a man immediately below her skirts, blushed furiously and turned away, going back up the companion to the deck. He approached the Mate.

'I gave Mrs Landon the message, sir. She said you were not to worry.'

Patience's face darkened. 'The devil she did.' He moved for the companionway; there was a lithe, catlike quality in his gait, a panther stalking its prey. He vanished and Tom heard him call in a thick voice, 'Mary!' Then there was silence until the name was repeated.

From below Mary Landon called back, 'Yes, what is it?'

'Mary, come up.'

'Really, I—'

'I said, come up. Come up this instant or I'll come down myself and get you.'

There was another silence, then Tom heard the sound of feet on the iron rungs of the vertical ladder. A few moments later there was a crash as someone, presumably the Mate, sent the tween-deck hatch-cover down with a bang to seal off the ladder and store below.

Then Mary Landon's voice, frigid: 'What's the meaning of this, Mr Patience?'

'You've no business down there. That damned Frenchy—'

'I was simply taking him some wine, nothing more than that. With my husband's approval.'

'Oh. Because he saved your life, I suppose.' The Mate's voice was thicker than ever, and now there was a note of sarcasm as well. 'I'm thinking the Captain's dispensation extended only so far as giving the Frenchy wine, Mary. Nothing else.'

'What do you mean by that?' The tone was cutting, and there had been a curious intensity in Mary Landon's voice, a sound of shock, of loathing, of hard anger.

Patience said, 'You know very well what I mean,' and his voice, too, was not normal. 'Mary, I can't help it...' After that there was a muffled sound, a sound as of a voice being stifled, and Tom believed the Mate had kissed Mary Landon. Hard on the heels of this sound there came another: an unmistakable slap. From the sharp noise it must have been a painful one.

For the rest of that morning the crew found out what hazeing really meant when performed by an expert.

'I'm sorry, Captain, but there it is. Impossibilities, miracles if you like, simply cannot be done.' The British consul, a Brazilian, spread his hands wide, shrugged, and smiled placatingly across his desk. 'There is not a British seaman available. It so happens that way. Those that were available a few days ago have signed aboard other ships.' He added, 'There are other nationalities, Dutchmen, Italians...'

'Thank you, no.' Landon picked up the tall hat that he had placed by his feet. 'I'll not bother you further. If I have to sail a man short, then so be it. As to the second replacement, I shall be bringing—'

'A moment, Captain, before you go. There is something I had almost forgotten.'

The consul fished in a drawer and brought out a letter with an official heading. 'The PSNC's *Orcoma* entered with mail from England.' He paused. 'There's a report of a man wanted by the police in Liverpool. You are out of Liverpool...it concerns a desertion, a Frenchman. The name is...' The consul read farther down the letter. 'Fontanet. Michel Fontanet.'

'H'm.' Landon was non-committal.

'I have stowaways in mind, of course.' The consul, a short, plump man of much self-importance went on, 'I know you'd have reported a stowaway if you had one, but I must make the formal enquiry all the same. You'll understand that.'

'Yes,' Landon said. He should have reported the stowaway immediately but had preferred to raise the question of replacements first; he had felt strongly that if he wished for a point to be stretched in his favour to the extent of signing on a stowaway rather than land him, his chosen order of things would make the transaction a shade easier in official eyes. It was a simple matter of psychology.

He asked casually, 'As a matter of interest, Mr Tavares. What is so special about this Frenchman that a letter should be sent from England? Deserters are—'

'The Liverpool police want him as I have said, that is the urgency. It is a case of murder.'

## CHAPTER 9

The man named Michel Fontanet had killed the Mate of his ship, smashing his head in with a fire hatchet whilst in port. Or so it was believed: there had in fact been no witnesses but there had been friction between Fontanet and the Mate and Fontanet had disappeared after the murder had been committed. Officially he was wanted for questioning only but, the consul had said, there was little doubt as to his guilt.

In terminating the interview without mention of a stowaway Landon was aware that, if as seemed only too likely, Chardonnet and Fontanet were one and the same, he was committing himself to a charge of aiding a criminal to escape, to say nothing of failing to report a stowaway. But the Frenchman had saved his wife's life and that weighed heavily in Landon's mind. As he walked away towards the docks Landon reflected that there could be coincidence around: Chardonnet had claimed to have deserted his ship not in Liverpool but in Dublin. The consul had given the name of the ship aboard which the murder had been committed and it was not, as claimed by Chardonnet, the *Aveyron*. But this proved little; Chardonnet—or Fontanet—would naturally have been covering his tracks as best he could.

Landon took out a large white linen handkerchief and, removing his tall hat, wiped his forehead. Sweat ran down his back beneath the thick pilot cloth. Recife was a stifling town, a mere eight degrees south of the Equator, and the starch in Captain Landon's collar and cuffs was becoming soggy as he walked through the palm-lined *plazas,* past the profusions of mimosa, myrtle and bombax. Moving with strangely dragging feet he reached the *Pass of Drumochter* and climbed the accommodation ladder rigged on the starboard side aft. Patience, still working cargo, saw him, seemed about to leave his work and come aft, but changed his mind. Landon went into the saloon and laid his tall hat on the settee, shaking his head gloomily.

'Mary,' he called.

There was no answer. Frowning, Landon went across to the door of the cabin. Mary was lying on the bunk, a damp linen cloth over her forehead. Her face was pale and Landon believed she had been crying. 'Why, my dear,' he said gruffly. 'What's the matter? Is it a headache?'

She nodded, wincing.

'It's the stuffiness. Never mind—we'll be away to sea quite shortly.' Pulling at his whiskers he looked down anxiously at his wife. 'You're sure it's no more than a headache, Mary?'

'Quite sure,' she answered with a touch of tartness. 'I'll be all right presently. I'd sooner be left alone for a while, Theodore.'

'I think you should take advantage of being in port to see a doctor. It's a long way, round Cape Horn—'

'It's nothing but a headache. I don't need a doctor.'

'Very well, then.' Landon hesitated. 'I have to talk to you, Mary. It's important. I'm sorry, but it won't wait.'

Her pallor seemed to deepen and there

was a shudder in her body. In a low voice she asked, 'Is it about the Frenchman?'

'Yes,' Landon answered in surprise. 'What made you ask that?'

Her eyes searched his face and he fancied that for some reason there was a touch of relief in her expression, but all she said was, 'Oh...only that you went ashore to make your report about him. Have you signed him on?'

'I have not,' he said shortly. 'But I intend to sail with him.'

She was puzzled; not a man to use easy phrases or to wrap up facts he told her what the consul had said. 'I know the name is different and so is the ship, but he would naturally alter that though he could scarcely disguise that he was a Frenchman. It would also be impossible to disguise that he was a seaman.'

She was staring at him as if she had seen a ghost. She said, 'I can't believe this! I can't believe he's a murderer. Theodore, if *you* believe it...why do you keep him aboard?'

He bent and kissed her on the cheek, gently. 'God forgive me for it, but he saved your life, my dearest girl, and it's not in me to hand him over to be hanged now.

I'm asking you to understand. To give me your support. Will you?'

He felt the shiver that ran through her body as he took her and gathered her into his arms. She said in a voice little above a whisper, 'The man will be a millstone. You can't carry him round the world indefinitely—sooner or later he must be handed over, either in Chile or Australia. Or Liverpool when we get back.' She was thoroughly alarmed now. 'Surely you can see?'

'I am already committed. I made no report.'

'But it's not too late—'

'No, Mary. I shall not hand him over—that's final, d'you hear me?' He was still holding her, and now he held her tighter, and she felt the urgency vibrant in his body. She felt he must be taking leave of his senses but knew she was powerless to make him change his mind. He went on with passion, 'I need your support, Mary. I must have it. I am committed and determined. But I need that.'

'Think, Theodore, please only *think!*'

'Say you give me your support.'

She was crying openly now, uncontrollably; but she gave a nod. Landon got to his feet, feeling drained, breathing hard. 'This will be between you and me alone for the time being, Mary. I'll say nothing yet to Patience. If word should spread before we leave Recife that we have a murderer aboard, I would lose hands I can't spare. Now rest yourself, my dear—and get rid of that headache.'

He turned away and going out on deck walked for'ard towards Number One hatch where he spoke to Patience.

'The Frenchman, Mr Patience. Is he still at work in the bosun's store?'

There was an odd look on the Mate's face. 'I'd not be surprised he is. I took the precaution of locking him in a while after you went ashore.'

'Why was that, Mr Patience?'

'I consider the man dangerous, sir, and didn't want him to skip. Besides...'

'Besides what?'

'The wine Mrs Landon took to him. With respect, I thought such a thing unwise. Who knows what effect—'

'It was by my own wish.'

'I know that.'

'*Has* it had any effect, Mr Patience?'

The Mate shrugged; there was a touch of insolence. 'I don't know. If I were you...I'd ask Mrs Landon that.'

Landon showed his astonishment in his face. 'What the devil d'you mean by that?'

'Just that she was in the store quite a while,' Patience said mendaciously. 'But that's not my business, is it?' He turned away. Landon caught him by the shoulder and swung him round.

'No, Mister, it is not. I'll not have such talk—'

'Talk, Captain? Who's said anything, beyond the stating of a fact?' Patience was sneering now.

'You know very well what I mean. It's not a good thing for the Master and First Mate of a ship to have bad blood between them, but I warn you, I shall not stand for your damnable insinuations.' Landon was bristling with anger; he looked formidable, and Patience flinched, as though expecting to be knocked to the deck. 'Go back to your duties, Mister.'

Patience went; it was never a good sign when the Old Man used the plain 'Mister'. Landon stood for a moment watching, then turned away and strode aft, deep anger quickening his steps. Reaching the saloon he said nothing to Mary; he had no wish to upset her further and would not have dreamed of insulting her by so much as mentioning what Patience had hinted at and thereby giving it some sort of implicit credence.

The mail came aboard at last, brought by an aged Brazilian driving a mule-cart, the animal wearing a grotesque straw hat against the fierce tropic sun. Tom found it a curious sight with the great ears sticking through holes cut in the straw. When the hands were sent to dinner at eight bells Mr Patience distributed the letters brought by the *Orcoma*. There was one for Jim Wales and one for Tom, not from his father but from his sister Susan.

It was discursive but brought welcome news of home.

Their father had as usual been busy with diocesan work; it was some while since brother Edward had written but he was known always to be much engrossed in his parish. Susan wrote of brother Philip on the North-West Frontier of India:

Yesterday a letter came from Philip. His regt. has been in action against the unruly Pathans. His head seems full of fighting

& thoughts of glory!!! He writes much of the Empire & the way in which the dear Queen's rule is being so greatly extended & the welcome which the blacks everywhere give to our soldiers, except of course those they are fighting!!! (She ended) Father sends his fondest love & hopes you are not finding your new life too hard. He remarked only today that we should no longer grumble about the rain which is as incessant as ever since you must have worse to put up with.

Ever yr. loving Sister,

Susan Chatto.

Tom grinned to himself as he put the letter back in its envelope and shut it in his sea-chest. He was fond of his sister, was closer to her than to either of his two brothers or his father, but already he felt there was a world between them since he'd left the deanery at Moyna. With the exception of his first night aboard and again during that horrible bout of seasickness, he'd not had any twinges of homesickness and now the whole life of the deanery, the holiday pursuits that had been such a pleasure to him only recently, had receded into a vague shadowy background that seemed quite unreal and even to have no significance when set against the world of men and hardships and vital tasks that was now his.

After the mid-day meal Tom scribbled a few lines in answer to the letter, intending to post his reply in Recife that night, when shore leave would presumably be given after the day's work was done and the decks cleared up.

But this was not to be. For some reason not yet given, Landon had decreed that all hands were to remain aboard for so long as the ship was in the port.

'Not like him,' Wales said. 'He's usually very good about shore leave—has a damn sight more sense than to keep men cooped up like chickens.' He added, 'There'll be trouble with the fo'c'sle crowd over this.'

Wales was right; all that afternoon the hands rumbled with discontent and Patience had to use his fists to keep them working. Then word spread that the Old Man was taking the Frenchy on with the ship around the Horn. No one saw any connection between Chardonnet and the cancellation of shore leave; but nevertheless, at three bells in the first dogwatch a deputation waited upon the Master, assembling on deck below the break of the poop.

Landon listened to them courteously, nodding in agreement when the point was made that the men were faced with a long, hard haul around Cape Horn and would not touch land again for many weeks, not until they made Valparaiso.

'I'm sorry,' Landon said, 'but I shall not allow shore leave and that is all there is to say—except that you know we are already two men short—'

'One?' came a loud voice. 'You're carrying the bloody Frenchy on.'

Landon said, 'Yes, that is true. One short, then. That is bad enough when heading down for the east-west passage of the Horn. I can find no replacements and I am not taking the risk of men deserting. That is final. Tonight Mr Patience will post a guard on the poop and fo'c'sle to ensure that my order holds. If any man has letters for the mail ship to England, they may hand them to Mr Patience, who will see that they go ashore after we have watered and provisioned tomorrow forenoon. Thereafter we sail at noon.'

Landon turned away and went below.

No one was inclined to believe that his given reason—thought strictly valid—was the real one.

In fact, it was not. Landon could not risk word being passed ashore that the ship had a Frenchman stowed away aboard. That night the fo'c'sle was loud with condemnation of Landon, the half-deck also being critical if less vociferous. Jim Wales, however, took positive steps to fill in an empty evening. He spoke to the bosun, and O'Connor went along to talk to the hands, and after a while they began drifting out on deck. Able Seaman Finney climbed onto the capstan with his fiddle and began playing the same shanty that he'd played on the Mate's order back in the Mersey.

One or two men took up the words and sang, at first without much heart.

'I stand on deck, my dearie, and in my
    fancy see
The faces of the loved ones that smile
    across the sea;
Yes, the faces of the loved ones, but midst
    them all so clear
I see the one I love the best, your bonnie
    face my dear.'

But when they had warmed up, the chorus came out strongly:

'And it's home, dearie, home! Oh, it's home I want to be,
My tops'ls are hoisted and I must out to sea,
For the oak, and the ash, and the bonnie birchen tree
Are all a-growing green in the North Countree...'

As the shanty ended Tom saw that the afterguard was coming on deck, all of them, Landon and his wife, Patience, Underwood and the steward, Vidler. When Finney struck up the next one they all joined in. They sang 'Away for Rio', 'Blow the Man Down' and many others. As the evening darkened and Tom, looking up, saw the moonlight silvering the masts and yards, he heard more singing coming from aft of them where a steamer was berthed. The steamer's crew was joining in, perhaps nostalgically thinking of their own days in sail—the days, as Patience put it caustically later, before they had left the sea and gone into steam.

In its way it was quite an evening and the men turned in a shade less bloody-mindedly than might otherwise have been the case. Only Horatio Mainprice had stood aloof from the impromptu sing-song and when the apprentices went back to the half-deck they found him scowling over a letter he was writing.

Wales asked, 'Why did you cry off, nipper?'

'Oh, I had better things to do.'

Wales reached out and laid hold of Mainprice's ear, giving it a sharp twist. Mainprice yelped like a puppy. 'Aboard a ship, the better thing is always to help keep up the crew's spirits. That's part of an officer's job. In addition to which, nipper, you'll not be cheeky in your answers to me. Have you got that?'

'Oh...*yes!*'

'And don't whine.' Wales let the ear go and Mainprice rubbed it vigorously. Muttering away to himself he went on with his letter. There was a good deal of tearing up of paper going on and the youth's bunk looked like a waste-paper basket. Before Wales ordered the dousing of the oil-lamp, Tom lay in his own bunk re-reading his sister's letter; when he thought about it, and about Susan herself, and visualized the big, rambling deanery, he began to see in the rather clumsy sentences a brave attempt to hide loneliness. He remembered how eagerly Susan had always welcomed him home from boarding school; now that he had really left home, now that he would re-appear in her life only once every couple of years or so, and briefly, she would miss him tremendously. It must be a complete change in her life, and no doubt the deanery would be a dreary place, inhabited as it was now by one old man and the servants. Tom wondered how Susan would fill her days; she was distinctly in danger of becoming that sad thing, a spinster, devoting her life to an elderly father. Little by little she would become wrapped up in diocesan affairs. There were few young men in the West of Ireland these days, and few to come into her life other than a handful of curates, and Tom could have wished his sister a better fate than to become a parson's wife...

Soon he fell asleep.

In the morning the hands were roused out early, ready to take on the maximum possible amount of stores and fresh water to last them for the long haul round Cape Horn and up the South American coast for Valparaiso. Barrel after barrel of salt horse, cask after cask of water were brought aboard and stowed after the water tanks themselves had been topped up from lighters; ships' biscuits and flour was checked aboard by the steward together with such fresh vegetables and fruit as could be obtained. This latter would not last long but at least it would help to ward off the scurvy that would be a possible danger in the later stages of the voyage. Also to combat the scurvy, much limejuice was embarked. The hen coops were topped up, some of the inmates having succumbed during the run from Liverpool with a consequent reduction in the daily quota of eggs. Also, the pig pen had lost one of its number; but this loss could not be made good in Recife.

Shortly before the decks were cleared up the Mate gave a shout for outgoing letters to be handed to him. Patience scanned the addresses briefly and, Tom thought, impertinently. Horatio Mainprice had written three. One was to his parents in Southsea, Hampshire. The Mate read out the other two in a mocking tone.

172

'Vice-Admiral Sir William Bloody Rivers, my word—Branston Hall, Petersfield, Hampshire. And what's this one?' Mr Patience's eyes seemed to rocket from his head as he looked at the third letter. 'The Lords Commissioners of the Admiralty! Lords Commissioners! What's all this about, boy?'

Horatio didn't appear to mind. With a superior smile he said, 'I'm applying to join the Royal Naval Reserve, sir.'

'What the hell for, boy?'

'That was Captain Landon's advice, sir,' Horatio said primly.

'Was it indeed. You don't imagine they're likely to look at an apprentice, do you?'

'Possibly not, sir. Which is why I've written also to Sir William Rivers, Sir.'

'Favouritism—hey? Do you know something, boy?'

'What, sir?'

'This: I don't give a donkey's arse for the Lords Commissioners of the Admiralty, who for my money wouldn't be able to hoist a fig-leaf in a gentle breeze. But I'd be mightily surprised if the buggers took any more kindly to that sort of bum-sucking than I would myself. Still, it's your letter.' He shrugged.

'Yes, sir,' Horatio said, his face flushed. 'As you say, it's my letter. And when I've obtained a commission in the RNR, sir, I shall use it to transfer to the RN itself—where at least the officers are gentlemen. Sir.'

Patience gave a start of sheer surprise, surprise that completely inhibited his tongue. Never in all his years at sea had he been spoken to in such a manner by anybody, least of all a pea-green youth from the half-deck. He took a step forward, still speechless though his face spoke for him loud and clear. Mainprice gave a kind of squeak and spun round and ran for his very life. There was a gale of laughter along the deck. Patience yelled after the fleeing boy, 'When we reach the pitch of the Horn, Mr *Midshipman* Mainprice, you'll be seeing for yourself the bloody wind doesn't give a fish's tit in hell whether or not you're in Debrett...just so long as you have the guts to climb out along an ice-bound yard!'

At eight bells the steam tug appeared with its belching black smoke and the ropes were cast off from the jetty. Once again the *Pass of Drumochter* was towed to sea, where she quickly picked up a wind and, her sails hoisted to the yards and trimmed to the breeze, turned south to pick up the trade-winds, the south-easterlies into which she would beat until she was around twenty degrees south of the line. Once the tug had taken off the pilot and was heading back into Recife, Landon set word for Chardonnet to be brought to the saloon. The Mate came in with the Frenchman, who was looking apprehensive though he still moved with his usual swaggering bounce.

Landon, otherwise alone in the saloon, said, 'Thank you, Mr Patience.'

'You don't wish me to stay?'

'Thank you—no.'

'I don't trust the man, sir, as well you know.'

'Quite, Mr Patience. I'm aware of your views. If you would be so kind as to leave, I'm confident I shall be in no danger.'

When Patience had gone, Landon, his hands clasped behind his broad back, took a turn or two up and down the saloon. There was a silence broken only by the small but continual creaking noises of a ship at sea and the more distant sounds from the rigging. Landon turned slowly and faced the Frenchman. 'Chardonnet,' he said, 'or Fontanet, Michel Fontanet. Which should it be?'

The man's face tightened but he shrugged, lifting his palms.

'I do not understand, *m'sieur.*'

'Oh, I think you do.' Landon stared the man in the eyes. 'Come now! I want the truth and I shall have it. You are Michel Fontanet, are you not?'

'*Mais non, m'sieur—*'

'But I think it should be *oui, m'sieur.* Listen to me, Fontanet. I have been ashore, I have spoken to our consul in Recife. I know the facts. You cannot hide anything now. I know you are facing a charge of murder.' Landon loomed over the man, thick and tall and still immensely strong despite his years. He had no weapon and he felt the need of none. He had the measure of the man. Chardonnet, or Fontanet, was lithe enough, and fit, but he was willowy, his body slightly built. And at the moment there appeared to be no fight in him at all; he had started to shake and was reaching out to clutch for support at the saloon table.

'Sit down,' Landon ordered. The Frenchman did so. 'The truth, now.

176

It's too late for lies, Fontanet. You must have realized that the news of the murder would have reached the British consuls at all foreign ports.'

The man had had the wind knocked right out of his sails. In a low voice he said, *'M'sieur.* I do not understand. If you know, why am I here still?'

Landon gave a short laugh. 'Only because I'm a fool, I think.' He paused, made a gesture with his hands. 'I could not bring myself to be the means of your hanging—richly though you deserve it if what I've been told is true. You saved my wife's life at sea. As a sailor as well as a husband, Fontanet, I know the full worth of what you did.'

The Frenchman said nothing. Landon said, 'Now. The story in full. Leave nothing out.'

The man still sat in silence, staring at the saloon's deck, hands twining and untwining. A shaft of sunlight coming through a port touched his head, brought up the rich brown lights in his hair. He would be an attractive man, Landon thought suddenly, to a woman...as this thought came the Frenchman began speaking in a high, rushing voice, largely in

French. Landon slowed him peremptorily: he must try to tell his story in English. Soon Landon was able to form a picture, one much as he had expected, of a hell-ship commanded by a drunken master and ruled and driven in total fear by a mate of the worst kind. Fontanet told a story of filthy, bug-infested accommodation, starvation provisions, slave wages, gear aloft rotten to the point of death to the men, and of savage, bestial cruelty on the part of the First Mate. Fontanet had seen men, he said, triced up in the fore rigging, stripped naked, flogged and then cut down and virtually skinned alive with deck scrapers. He had seen arms and legs broken and ribs stove in—not by the force of surging water or falls from aloft, but by the brute strength of the Mate's own hands, more often than not backed up by an iron belaying-pin.

It was a terrible story. Landon offered no comment as yet. Fontanet went on, 'I was maddened, *m'sieur*, I was scarcely responsible for what I did. To talk about it now in cold blood...*M'sieur*, the day this took place the Mate had most brutally refused a young sailor permission to go ashore to see his wife, who was in labour and very sick...and then the Mate pounded this young man to a pulp.' Fontanet looked down at the deck. 'I think I did not know what I was doing, *m'sieur*. That night I found the Mate alone on deck... I picked up a fire hatchet, and I killed him, and ran from the ship.'

'All this is the truth?' Landon asked harshly.

'It is the truth, *m'sieur*.'

'You swear it?'

The Frenchman placed his right hand over his heart. 'I swear this by the Holy Virgin.'

Landon nodded. 'Then under British law it is possible...but I can make no promises and would not wish to raise your hopes too high.' Extreme provocation, if proved, might perhaps reduce the charge to manslaughter but Landon was no lawyer. He resumed his pacing. He was prepared to believe Fontanet's story, had in fact no doubt he had got the truth. But heavy problems loomed ahead. He went on, 'You've done a terrible thing...yet you do not look to me a bad man in your heart, and I am well accustomed to judge men's characters. Also I know there are many such bucko mates as you have described.'

He paused, then said briskly, 'Well—we shall see. In the meantime I shall continue working you with the hands and there will be no talk of murder—you have my promise. On your part, you'll promise me that you'll keep your temper under control aboard my ship.'

When Fontanet had left the saloon—and before he left, Landon had told him he would continue to be known aboard as Paul Chardonnet—the First Mate had appeared with such indecent haste that for a moment Landon wondered if he had been listening at the skylight on the poop; but the sheer unsatisfied curiosity in Patience's face convinced the Captain that this was not the case. With an abrupt lack of courtesy Patience demanded, 'Well, sir? What had he to say for himself?'

'A private conversation, Mr Patience.' Landon felt unaccustomedly awkward in Patience's presence; for the first time in his career he was deliberately withholding from an officer information that that officer had every right to know. 'I can add only that I am still happy to carry him on.'

'I don't like it. I don't like it at all. And I'll have his hide, so help me God, if he gives any sort of trouble!'

Landon said sharply, 'You'll treat him no differently from any other of the men—there will be no picking on him. That is an order. See that you obey it.'

The Mate's face reddened but after a moment he relaxed and said grudgingly, 'Oh, I'll obey it, of course. I know my duty. But you mark my words, Captain—that damned Frenchy's going to bring trouble to the ship.'

Patience turned and stamped out of the saloon.

In the privacy of the sleeping-cabin that night, when the *Pass of Drumochter* was tacking south into the trades and all was well on deck, Landon spoke of his dilemma. 'Possibly I should have taken Patience into my confidence, Mary. He has a right.'

She touched his cheek tenderly. 'A right which I'm sure he'd prefer not to exercise, Theodore.'

He pondered. 'You mean, the responsibility's now mine alone? But the final responsibility is always the Master's.'

'But if he had been party to this...surely

there's a difference...in a criminal court he too would be looked upon as an accessory. At least,' she added, 'that's what I would think.'

'That's splitting hairs, Mary. If he'd refused to agree, which he would, and had I then ordered him to work Fontanet with the others, my order would have removed his personal responsibility. He'd have made an official protest and demanded that I enter it in the log. I could not legally have refused.' Landon sighed, shifted restlessly. 'I think, now, that I should have given him the chance.'

'Then why did you not?'

He answered simply, 'There would have been a great deal of unpleasantness all round. I had no wish to upset the crew and I believed that once Patience knew, then it would be impossible to prevent a further spread of rumour. I felt that the well-being of the ship and crew should be my first consideration.'

'Then leave things just as they are,' Mary said decisively. 'I think you've made the right decision—over *that* point. But oh, Theodore, why did you not heed what I said? Why did you bring that man on? There's going to be so much trouble eventually and I shall be dreading our arrival in Valparaiso.'

Landon sighed again. 'It's a long way yet to Valparaiso, Mary.'

## CHAPTER 10

The steady south-east trades took the *Pass of Drumochter* down to around twenty degrees south latitude, and brought much work to the hands as the ship changed constantly from one tack to another; and the watch on deck was sent time and again to the braces for trimming the yards. The ship needed much careful attention and the first-voyage apprentices learned a good deal about the difficult art of handling a sailing ship to full advantage; and when possible their education in navigation, begun during the time spent in the Doldrums before Recife, was continued by the Second Mate.

Tom asked about the trade winds. 'What's the reason they blow the way they do, sir?'

'Never heard of Buys-Ballot's law,

evidently. Well, that law states the relation between the direction of the wind and that of the barometric gradient. For instance...in the northern hemisphere, if you stand with your back to the wind, the centre of lowest pressure will be on your left, in a direction that makes an acute angle with the way the wind's blowing. It's the exact opposite in the southern hemisphere, which is what we're in now of course. In accordance with Buys-Ballot, the wind blows spirally inwards towards the centre of a cyclonic system, and spirally outwards from an anti-cyclonic system. D'you follow—or not?'

Tom answered doubtfully. 'I think I do.'

Underwood laughed. 'Like hell you do! Listen, young Chatto, never be afraid to say you don't understand. You'll never learn, otherwise. Now: the what-you-might-call *permanency* of the trades is due to the particular distribution of barometric pressure in a high-pressure belt that encircles the globe at the tropics, both north and south of the line...whilst over the line itself and its immediate vicinity the pressure is *less*—to the extent of around a fifth of an inch maybe. And in obedience to old Buys-Ballot, Chatto, permanent winds blow from these high-pressure areas towards the low pressure which constitutes what we call the equatorial trough—hence causing the north-east trades in the Tropic of Cancer and the south-east trades down here in Capricorn. All right?'

'I think I see,' Tom said. It was still hazy. 'What happens when we leave the trades behind, sir?'

'We pick up the north-westerlies, the anti-trades.'

'Anti...and yet they blow us the same way still?'

'With tacking, yes, they do. That's where the skill of the Old Man comes in. The trick is to get the ship to lie as close to the wind as possible. Some do, some don't. Masters vary. Captain Landon's first-class, but I've known better sailers than the *Pass of Drumochter*...anyway, later on still, we'll pick up the Roaring Forties...they blow below forty south, often down to below the Horn, and they're from the west. It's into the Roaring Forties we have to beat to get around Cape Horn—right into the teeth of them. I've known ships take six weeks to get round, tacking up and down, up and down...waiting for the shift that'll take them through.' He grinned. 'It's a real bastard right enough, when it's like that. But maybe we'll be lucky this time, you never know with the Horn.'

Tom, after some seven weeks at sea now, had never felt healthier. He was full of energy in spite of the inadequate food; his muscles were firm and strong and he was putting on good firm flesh as well. His eyes were clear, his skin tanned by wind and weather and sunlight. He loved the feel of the wind in his hair, blowing out his clothing, blowing away all the festooning cobwebs of the land. It was a joy to go aloft and lay out along the yards with the men, feeling a man himself, doing a man's job in a man's world, becoming more and more sure-footed as the days passed. It was a pleasure to welcome each new morning as the ship thrust south for the Horn, through deep blue seas that seemed to reach to the very ends of the earth—sea and sky and cloud, and white canvas, and sailormen, and nothing else, no land anywhere.

Tom gloried in it all.

Chardonnet was taking frequent tricks at the wheel and often Landon was on the poop to watch him. Landon, as the Second Mate once remarked to Tom, had a bee in his bonnet about good helmsmen and the training thereof. A good man at the wheel was worth his weight in gold and Landon was set upon having the Frenchman fully conversant with the whims of the *Pass of Drumochter* by the time the ship was down into the high south latitudes.

One day when Chardonnet had been at the wheel Horatio Mainprice came into the half-deck with a sly look, a knowing grin and an air of furtive excitement. He said, 'D'you know something?'

'What?' Tom asked.

'I'd bet my last sovereign,' the junior apprentice said, 'there's going to be murder done aboard this ship before much longer.'

'Oh, yes?' Wales, who had been burrowing in his sea-chest, straightened. 'What's all this about, then, nipper?'

'Well, I was overhauling the ratlines on the mizzen shrouds...I couldn't help overhearing—I didn't really listen, of course—'

'Of course.'

'Patience was on watch and the Frenchy was at the wheel...the Old Man's wife was on the poop as well. She was talking to the Frenchy, and laughing. Really friendly.' Horatio's eyes were round and staring. 'You could have cut the atmosphere with a knife—Patience was furious. In the end he bawled at the Frenchy to keep his eye lifting on the weather leech of the main t'gallnts'l, though so far as *I* could see we were as close to the wind as we're ever likely to get. The Frenchy's good on the wheel, I'll say that,' Mainprice added with all the authority of two months' sea-time behind him; Tom grinned, meeting Wales' eye. 'The thing is, the Frenchy answered him back. As good as told him to piss off.'

'So what happened?' Wales asked.

'Patience had him relieved from the wheel, sharp. I thought for a moment the Mate was going to smash Chardonnet's face in...but he sent him to the foremast crosstrees and said he'd to stay there till he apologized.' Mainprice paused. 'What Patience actually said was, till he bloody well crawled.'

'And the Old Man? What did he have to say about it?'

'I don't know. Patience sent me down before the Old Man came up.'

Wales nodded, and turned back to his

sea-chest. 'Don't get too excited over that sort of thing, nipper. It doesn't make life easier for anybody, and there's just one person likely to get really hurt and that's the Old Man. Rumour has it that he brought Chardonnet on in spite of opposition from Patience.'

'Yes, I—'

'So can't you see what a position this puts the Old Man in—or might, in time?'

'Yes,' Horatio said with a snigger. 'Specially if the Old Man's wife comes into it.'


Doggedly Patience said, 'You should never have carried him on, sir. Don't say I never told you.'

'That's not the point, Mr Patience—'

'Oh? Then what is?'

Landon held on to his temper. 'Mr Patience, do not be impertinent. I am backing you, as back you I must. If the man was inattentive to his duty, then he had to be punished—I would expect no less. But what is going to happen if he refuses to—*crawl* was I believe the word you used?'

Patience snapped. 'Why, then he'll stay where he is, come wind and weather.'

'Oh, no. I think not.'

Patience gaped. 'What did you say, Captain?'

Landon said tautly, 'I have never run a hell-ship, Mr Patience, nor a down-easter. I do not propose to approach the high south latitudes with a man upon the crosstrees, and that is final.'

Patience breathed hard but said, 'Oh he'll come to his senses before then you may be sure.'

'That remains to be seen.' Landon felt a sudden fury towards Patience, who had placed him in such a predicament by his precipitate action. Mary had told him the man had been steering a proper course and had been fully alive to the set of the canvas. He snapped, 'You're in a fair way to showing yourself up before the hands as a fool, Mr Patience, a man who makes idle threats and has to eat his words—'

'Captain, I—'

Landon held up a hand. 'A moment, Mr Patience. Crawl or not, Chardonnet is coming down from aloft within twelve hours, and sooner if the weather conditions should make it necessary.'

The Mate gave a gasp. 'Are you saying

you'd let me down before the fo'c'sle gang, sir?'

Landon spread his hands. 'The remedy lies with you alone, Mr Patience. You must find a way of saving your face.'

'By God!' Patience shouted. 'I'll kill him first!' He stormed out of the saloon and went for'ard to the fo'c'sle-head and stood there in the eyes of the ship, close to the bowsprit, arms folded across his chest, glaring with furious eyes into the crosstrees. Tom, working on deck, watched him and glanced aloft in time to see Chardonnet blow the Mate what looked very much like a kiss...there was a shout of rage from the fo'c'sle and the Mate came bounding down the starboard ladder and raced for the foremast shrouds.

There was going to be real trouble now: Tom recalled what Horatio Mainprice had said so recently. He didn't linger. He ran for the saloon and burst unceremoniously through the door. Landon and his wife stared as though he had gone crazy.

'Sir—'

'What's the meaning of this, young man?'

Tom explained, his words tumbling over each other. Landon's face was formidable.

191

He said, 'Stay here, boy,' and, pushing Tom aside, ran from the saloon. A moment later Tom heard his strong voice calling for Patience to come down to the deck immediately. After that Tom found all his attention taken up by Mary Landon. Her face was as white as a sheet; tears ran down her cheeks. Her hands were clenching and unclenching at her sides. She made a move towards the door but Tom stopped her, sensing that Captain Landon would prefer her not to be on deck.

'Ma'am,' he said uncertainly, reaching out a hand. 'Please, ma'am, stay here till the Captain comes back.'

She gave a low sob, twisting a handkerchief in her fingers. She remained where she was, quivering, making no further attempt to leave. But what she said next hit Tom like the blow of a fist. She said passionately, 'They must be stopped, they *must!* A man who has killed once—'

Abruptly, she broke off, staring in alarm at Tom.

She was very upset. She had not, she said to Tom, fully realized what she had said nor did she know why she had said it. He was not to pay any attention to an unfortunate outburst. He had to promise—another promise!—not to say a word to anyone.

The promise given, Mary Landon went firmly to the saloon door and along the alleyway to the deck. Tom followed. From the waist they saw Landon standing by the break of the fo'c'sle with his head back, staring up at the foremast. Another man had reached the crosstrees and that man was speaking urgently to the First Mate, obviously trying to reason with him and at the same time restraining Chardonnet. The man was the carpenter, a trusted petty officer. Tom felt the rising tension as all eyes stared upward; Landon seemed to be concentrating everything into his eyes, as if trying to will the men aloft away from senseless violence; but was holding himself back from any vocal interference in case he should precipitate anything. Mary also was staring as if transfixed, hands clenched against her breasts. Aloft, the carpenter was still talking, with one hand firmly grasping the shrouds, the other keeping Chardonnet pinned on the side away from Patience.

Then, at last, Patience was seen to start down the lee shrouds.

Tom heard Mary Landon's gasp of relief, saw the quick gladness in the Captain's face.

The carpenter reached the deck on the weather side shortly after Patience stepped off the lee shrouds. He caught Mary Landon's eye. 'It'll be all right now, ma'am,' he said gently, and there was understanding in his expression. Mary flushed, and murmured her gratitude. Tom then heard Patience ordered to the saloon. Without a word Mary turned away aft and walked back towards the cabin. Tom carried on with his interrupted work. Five minutes later the bosun was sent for. He came out from the saloon and called aloft to Chardonnet.

'Down you come, Frenchy.'

Chardonnet came down with insolent slowness.

'Captain wants you in the saloon,' O'Connor said. 'So move yourself, all right?'

'You will apologize to Mr Patience,' Landon said formally, 'or you'll go aloft again and this time it'll be by my own order.' He looked the Frenchman in the eye, standing stiff and straight as a ramrod on the side of the saloon table opposite Chardonnet.

The Frenchman said nothing.

'I am waiting.'

'M'sieur, the Mate, he is a—'

'Don't be a fool, man! I am giving you a chance. Already you have deserted a ship...you will find me a hard man if you give trouble aboard my ship—and you can scarcely desert at sea unless you wish to provide food for the sharks!'

The Frenchman shrugged, looked sideways at the Mate, then back to the Master. 'To you, *m'sieur le capitaine,* I apologize—'

'To Mr Patience. This is your last chance.'

There was a pause, and a curious look passed briefly across Chardonnet's face. 'To *M'sieur* Patience also. I apologize.'

Landon glanced at the Mate, who gave a reluctant nod. There had been no crawling in Chardonnet's demeanour. Landon said crisply, 'Very well, Chardonnet, your apology is accepted. I warn you that if you repeat your conduct you'll be in much trouble—and when we berth in Valparaiso you'll be landed with a bad discharge. I think you know what that might mean?'

Chardonnet bowed his head. 'Yes, *mon capitaine*. There will be no trouble.'

When Chardonnet had been dismissed about his work Landon, seeing the look on the Mate's face, said sharply, 'You should be thankful for any settlement of the matter. This could have become more dangerous than I would ever have cared to contemplate.'

Patience swung away without a word and went rudely out of the saloon, banging the door to behind him. Landon sat, and found that his heart was pounding and his hands had an uncontrollable shake. Holding them up, he stared at them, and slowly shook his head. All at once he felt his age. He was a damned old fool to have brought the Frenchman on from Recife; if he hadn't known that before he could scarcely avoid being aware of it now. He had done nothing more than postpone the inevitable. There would be no alternative to an eventual handing over of Chardonnet.

Sighing, he crossed the saloon to the sideboard where bottles were stowed in racks. He poured himself a whisky, a small one. Landon was an abstemious man and especially so at sea, but today he needed the comfort and would have liked another tot.

'What's the matter with you, Chatto?' Mainprice asked.

Tom looked up. 'Nothing. Why?'

Horatio Mainprice pulled his shirt over his head, ready for his bunk. 'You look thoughtful,' he said.

'Somebody's got to think.' Tom was worried about what Mary Landon had said to him in the saloon and he'd done a lot of thinking about it all the rest of the day, though in truth it hadn't taken all that much thought to show him the basic fact that Mrs Landon must know something that no one else aboard, except no doubt Landon himself, knew; and since it was unlikely Mr Patience had murdered anyone it was obvious she'd been referring to the Frenchman.

It was scary to think that there was a murderer loose aboard, if Mrs Landon was right. Perhaps it would have been better if he hadn't said anything that night when the bosun had been busy with his belaying-pin; there might have been a certain justice in O'Connor's action. Whenever Tom saw the Frenchy now he would be speculating about what the man's hands might have done that Mrs Landon appeared to know about. But, a few days later, an incident occurred that at first disgusted and then much surprised him.

He was working on deck with Horatio Mainprice, under the carpenter, when a smallish creature, golden red with whirring, filmy wings, skimmed from the sea's surface, came over the bulwarks and flopped to the deck close to where the apprentices were working.

Horatio started. 'My God! What's that?'

'Flying fish, boy. Funny little creatures.' The carpenter was moving towards the fish with the obvious intention of dropping it back over the ship's side when Horatio Mainprice moved suddenly and brought his seaboot down on it, hard. There was a squishing sound and the guts spilled out on the deck. The little creature's mouth opened feebly, twice, and the broken wings, like the skeletons of leaves, twitched. Dabbs, the carpenter, looked as stunned, as dumbfounded as Tom had ever seen a man look. He took an angry step towards the apprentice but someone else got there faster: Chardonnet. The Frenchman had evidently been watching from aloft and now he came sliding at speed down the maintopmast staysail halliard, disdaining the shrouds.

He ran towards the dead fish and went down on his haunches. *'Merde!'* he said, staring up furiously at Mainprice. *'Le pauvre petit...'* Slowly he straightened. *'Pourquoi...pourquoi?'*

Horatio shrugged. *'Je ne sais pas,'* he answered indifferently. *'Mais je n'aime pas quelque chose qui me...'* His French ran out. 'I don't like things that startle me, that's all. I don't see what it's got to do with you anyhow.'

Chardonnet seemed near tears. *'Cochon!'* he said, and spat towards Mainprice, who dodged back angrily. Dabbs stepped in between them and put a hand on Chardonnet's arm. 'Easy, now,' he said quietly. 'Take it easy, matey, it's done and you can't undo it. You don't want any more trouble. Not over a fish.'

'But *m'sieur*—'

'Yes, sure, I know. He's a little bugger, but he'll learn. Off you go. Frenchy. Take my advice and leave it now.'

Dabbs kept his hand on the man's arm and his eyes steady on his face until he felt Chardonnet relax, then he let go. Chardonnet bent and gathered the fish gently into his hands, walked to the side and dropped the remains over the bulwarks. Then he went back aloft, climbing the shrouds slowly. Dabbs turned on Horatio. 'Don't ever do that again,' he warned solemnly. 'What's the sense in cruelty for its own sake, boy? If we had a starving crew who need it for their dinner...but we haven't. It's throwing God's goodness back in His face, boy, to destroy any life needlessly.'

It had been a nasty incident; but it had been Chardonnet who had impressed Tom. He began to think Mrs Landon couldn't have been right in what she'd hinted at. It could have been simply a rumour picked up in Recife.

Soon they were coming down the eastern coastlines of Uruguay and Argentina, well out to seaward to head down easterly past the Falkland Islands before swinging in towards Tierra del Fuego and the Horn itself. Before they reached fifty degrees south latitude, Landon had bent on the best suit of sails and had ordered the overhauling of all the gear. Already the masts had been tarred down—a filthy job and one that worsened the Mate's mood each time a drop fell on his decks from aloft—and on the foremast a cracked parrel, the metal band that held the yard to the mast whilst allowing it to travel up and down on the lifts, had been replaced. A good number of new footropes, buntlines, leechlines and gaskets had been rove in places missed during the last hurried overhaul before Recife; and all the seizings on the rigging lanyards had been carefully examined and made good where necessary.

When Patience had personally inspected everything he made his report to the Master. The ship was now as ready as it could be for the ordeal of the Horn.

By the time they had passed south of the 50th parallel real freezing cold began to invade the half-deck. Except for the galley and the saloon there was no warmth anywhere. The wind increased as they were hit by the westerlies' full ferocious force after they had fought their way south past the Falklands for the tip of the South American continent. That wind howled eerily through the rigging, sounding at times like a whole orchestra, at others like a pack of mad dogs. Now their world was one of continual storm conditions, of flung spray, of solid water that rushed foaming along the deck every time the ship put her nose beneath a sea and, but for the lifelines rigged fore and aft, would have swept every man to his death in a boiling sea.

No warmth: no dryness either.

Men on watch were soaked continually, and they stayed soaked when they went below. There was nowhere for drying out clothes other than the galley, which couldn't cope with everyone at once, and when the weather worsened, as it would, the galley and saloon fires would in any case be drawn.

As they neared Cape Horn and came into the greater force of wind sweeping unchecked right around the world's southern tip, the taking in of sail became a nightmare of danger and frustration as frozen hands reached for frozen canvas and frozen feet slipped about on ice-encrusted footropes high above the decks—decks that canted sharply so that at times the men aloft were working with the upper masts tilted to almost thirty degrees with the wind tearing at them all the while. The sky was continually overcast, with no chance now of sun sights or star sights to fix the ship's position. Gone were the golden days to the north, gone the idyllic feeling of being aloft above a blue sea with hurrying white clouds far overhead and a gentle breeze wafting around bared torsos. Now the sea was no place for a lover of comfort.

Horatio Mainprice's face grew pinched and white, or more often blue, and when he came down from aloft he flopped into his bunk all standing, wet through and shivering, to sleep at last the sleep of sheer exhaustion. Even Jim Wales grew bad-tempered and morose and snapped at the junior apprentices for no reason. It was the Cape Horn sickness, a sickness brought on in the mind by a deadly compound of cold, weariness, poor food and little of it, continual buffeting from wind and water, the horrible misty overcast, the cold fug below decks, and a heaviness of spirit due to the impression that—however many times it had in fact been done before—it simply was not possible to beat into those damned westerlies and make the passage of the dreaded Horn.

Landon was called when at seven bells one morning watch Patience made their dead-reckoning position as being nearly due east of the Horn and distant around forty miles, with the ship still on a southerly course. Landon came up on deck, water cascading from his sou'wester even before he had taken a couple of steps from the shelter of the companion.

'Good morning, Mr Patience.'

Patience grunted. 'Just look at it.'

'Worse than many passages I've known, but better than some.' Landon steadied himself against the rail and took a long look aloft. The *Pass of Drumochter* was moving on under the forecourse and reefed lower topsails only, and it was doubtful if more canvas would be sent up until they were safely round. He said, 'We'll try to beat to the west for a little, Mr Patience, and if that's no good, then we'll drop farther south and try for a shift there.'

'You'll not forget the pack-ice, sir?'

Landon gave him a brief look. 'No, Mr Patience, I'll not forget the pack-ice, you may be sure.'

He took another careful, narrow-eyed look aloft, stared into the wind as if trying to assess its intentions, then looked aft at the man at the wheel—Able Seaman Finney, the old shanty-man.

'You're all right, Finney?'

'Aye, sir.' Finney, chewing tobacco like

a cow chewing the cud, gripped the spokes firmly.

Landon frowned, held his face to the wind again, and said, 'I shall double-bank the helm from now on, Mr Patience. For now, for wearing ship, I'll have Chardonnet aft, if you please.'

'Chardonnet?' The Mate's jaw came forward. 'Finney can manage. If he can't, we have plenty—'

'Chardonnet, Mr Patience.'

'But—'

'*Do as you're told, Mister!*' It was an angry shout; even the Master was feeling the effects of the Horn's vicinity.

Patience shrugged angrily and snapped at Tom. 'You there, boy, fetch the Frenchy. Smart, now!'

Tom went for the ladder, made his way with difficulty along to the waist, breasting the torrent of water rushing down from for'ard, clinging hard to the lifeline. Constantly his sea-booted feet were swept from under his body and he hung from the lifeline like a fish from a hook, thrashing about, waiting for the water to drain away through the washports, then making a little more reeling progress, a series of dashes before the next sea thundered aboard over the plunging bow, currently headed direct for the southern ice.

Somehow he made the break of the fo'c'sle, waited till the deck was free of water, then flung the door open into the crew's accommodation. The stench was fearful; wet clothing, dirty bodies—no one was even thinking about washing now and hadn't done so for some days past—all the confined human smells of a crowded fo'c'sle messdeck hit him like a blow in the face. All those bodies looked dead rather than merely in a sleep of exhaustion. He located the Frenchman and moved towards his bunk and was about to reach out and shake him awake when the door came open again and the bosun entered. O'Connor, seeing Tom's action, shouted, 'All right, lad, leave him be. Come here a moment.'

Tom went across the lurching deck.

'Is Chardonnet wanted, boy?'

Tom nodded. 'For the wheel—'

'Right. Now—never you lay hands on a man when he's dead asleep,' the bosun said harshly. 'That's the rule at sea. Just make a racket, that's all. You touch a man, he's liable to lash out.' He lifted his voice. 'All hands,' he roared. 'All hands on deck—wear ship! Come on now, rouse out, you rotten lazy bastards, or you'll be feeling the weight of my boot up your perishing fat backsides. Frenchy—you're wanted on the poop to back up the wheel. Make it smart now.'

Tom left him to it and struggled back along the deck. As the hands tumbled out behind him he heard Landon's shouted order: *'Stand by to come about!'* Then he saw the Old Man nod at Patience and the Mate started for'ard for the fo'c'sle to take charge. When everyone was at his station Landon passed the orders.

'Ready-oh!' Then: *'Lee fore brace...hard up, the helm!'*

Chardonnet and old Finney struggled to bring the wheel round against the weather. After this the fore and head sheets were let go and then the next order came: *'Raise tacks and sheets.'* Bodies were everywhere, cursing, sliding, half drowning. The yards were coming round, so quickly now that it was the devil's own job to take up the slack of the braces sharp enough. Once the fore braces were in, the work of bracing up and belaying the yards began. The blocks of the headsheets thumped and banged along the deck until their racket was drenched by dropping tons of green, icy water. Tom, back on the poop now and waiting any orders from the Master, was flung bodily across the deck to fetch up hard against the coaming of the saloon skylight. For one terrible moment as he came free of the coaming he felt himself sliding down the angled deck, pushed by the weight of a sea towards the side; but he got a grip on the guardrail and hung with his body over the waves until the ship steadied and he was dropped back to the deck.

Landon glanced round. 'All right, Chatto?'

'I—I think so, sir.'

'Never move from one point till you know you can reach the next—that way, you'll stay alive.' Landon turned his attention back to the sails with one eye on the helm. Gradually, very gradually, the *Pass of Drumochter* came round into wind and weather, the yards being trimmed continually as she did so. Landon kept glancing at the wheel; Chardonnet, by far the stronger of the two helmsmen, was the guiding hand, and was performing skilfully, his whole attention concentrated on his job.

Coming round a little more, Landon held the ship for a while on the port tack, making an attempt to beat to windward for the passage of the Horn; but the ship made almost no progress throughout the next watch, nor any more when Landon put her about again onto the opposite tack. Later that day he made the decision that he must after all head farther south to seek out a shift in the wind even though this meant that they would be heading down for the ice. With the Frenchman once again on the wheel, Landon executed the difficult and dangerous manoeuvre of bringing the ship about so that the worsening weather would come onto her starboard quarter, the moment of most danger approaching when her head began to fall off the wind and sea and she started what felt to Tom like a wild and uncontrollable swoop away from the weather.

He was on the ice-covered main yard when the ship gave a convulsive shudder and lurch. Holding on desperately as the wind tore at his oilskin, he looked back at the most awesome sight he had ever seen. A huge wall of water had reared up, blotting out the sky, dwarfing the struggling ship, rising up way beyond the trucks of the masts, its breaking crest apparently about to drop with crushing tons of weight to smother and destroy. The ship was sliding bodily down the side of that immense wave, descending into the trough. A curious half-silence came down on the vessel as the wind was cut off by the solid wall of water; the weather sounds were distant now, and the sounds of ship and men became suddenly quite startlingly loud by comparison. Tom heard the creaking of the strained gear, and an ominous flap-flap from the canvas as the sails dropped, windless, against the masts. O'Connor was also on the main yard and when he spoke his voice was clear, perfectly audible without shouting, and yet oddly flat and muted.

'You'll need both hands for your life in a moment, boy,' he said. 'Now's when we may broach-to, if we're unlucky or the Old Man doesn't judge it just right...or if the Frenchy's slow to bring the helm up—or too quick!'

There seemed to be many chances of doom. O'Connor remarked that many a ship had been lost in the high south latitudes, lost with all hands and the cook as the saying went. 'But if all goes well, that sea'll pass beneath us. That's when you're going to need all your grip, boy.'

Looking out to leeward, Tom saw another great wall of water forming, reaching right into the overcast, lowering, grey sky and joining it to form what looked like one solid mass. The ship was right at the bottom of a canyon, closed right in, seeming helpless, totally vulnerable. Then Tom heard the bosun's indrawn breath; he glanced at him, saw the look of horror and fear in his face. O'Connor had involuntarily lifted an arm as though to ward off the crushing weight of water to come.

Tom turned and looked where the bosun was looking.

The huge wave was nearer, much nearer, and its crest seemed on the point of dropping down on the ship. Then there was a shout from aft.

'*Hard up, the helm! Lee fore brace!*'

On deck men threw their weight onto the braces and slowly, slowly, the yards came round, just a little; and then, as Tom expected the whole weight to topple, O'Connor let out his breath in a long gasp and said, 'It's all right now, boy.' All at once the *Pass of Drumochter* lifted, a tremendous surge of life sweeping through her and bringing her back from the dead, and the wave passed beneath her so that, instead of being in a canyon she shot to the heights and Tom, from the mainyard, looked sheer down the side of a water-mountain, with the ship once again in the grip and turmoil of the Roaring Forties and the sails straining out from the clews, stiff and taut as boards.

That night there was little sleep, and there would be little now until the ship had passed through the terrible Cape Horn winter, round into the South Pacific.

Continually now the cry was for All Hands; no sooner had Tom flopped exhausted and wet through into his bunk, the bedding of which was also soaked continually with salt water, than again the order would be shouted along the deck and weary, cursing men would turn out into the never-ending storm as Landon brought the ship onto another tack, searching and searching endlessly for the shift of wind that would take them in the right direction.

During one snatched period in the half-deck Ted Allan opened his heart to Tom. 'I've had about enough...it's a rotten life. This sort of thing, time and again, right through a man's life—and for what? Twelve quid a month for the

Master—twelve bloody quid! You need to be in love with the Line to do it for that money.'

'So it's back to the farm, is it?'

'Well—no. You still work all hours for a pittance. If it's not All Hands it's bloody lambs in the middle of the night.' He added, 'Trouble is, I'm blowed if I know *what* I want.'

Tom felt, not for the first time, that there was an indecisiveness about Allan that would in any case damage his chances at sea... Allan started talking again. 'I don't know how you do it. I mean, how you always manage to look cheerful and willing even when I bet you don't feel it. Helps, does that. Makes people *like* you.' He saw Tom's embarrassment; he stared at him for a moment, speculatively, then asked, 'What's your ambition, kid?'

Tom answered with simple directness, 'To command a ship. Isn't that the ambition of everyone who goes to sea as an officer?'

Allan laughed without humour. 'There's a devil of a way to go from apprentice to Master. I'm not sure I'd ever get there.' He hesitated, eyes large and questing in the thin, fair-skinned face. 'You know,

Chatto...a man finds out a hell of a lot about himself at sea. Things he didn't know before.' He stopped again and Tom believed he was about to elaborate but just then there was a shout along the deck outside and Allan groaned. 'Don't tell me I heard bloody Patience,' he said.

It was All Hands. Tom reached for his oilskin and sou'wester and they stumbled out again.

## CHAPTER 11

It became an automaton-like world, an existence of reflexes.

In the unremitting westerlies they dropped south, down to the fringes of the southern pack-ice, to the bastions of the Antarctic continent well below the Horn. Now snow and ice, flying slivers of pain and danger that cut blue, shivering flesh like glass, filled the very air.

Tom Chatto's mind seemed numb and useless, utterly beyond thought as he stared through the overcast and the driven snow at the heaving grey waste of sea. On and on, hour after hour, day after day until the days became weeks, the *Pass of Drumochter* made her terrible way up and down the world's worst area of storm, seeking, searching, waiting, hoping, with that constant cry of All Hands as Landon fancied he had the wind he needed to make his way west. But always it was the wrong one; ever and again the ship was driven back, forced to fall off the wind and try again.

Jodurecom, Tom thought, was all very well; Mr Ralph back in Liverpool ought to try the Horn for himself. Currently life was a misery of body and spirit. Tom thought with longing of home. Home was peace and tranquillity, and a warm bed, and a roaring fire, and well-cooked food, and safety. Perhaps he'd been a fool not to have heeded his father; brother Edward, comfortably enfolded in the arms of the Church, had chosen better. Edward's worst grumble would be about early service on a winter's morning.

'Come along—turnout, you bloody loafer.' There was anger in Jim Wales' voice; tempers had grown short by this time. The senior apprentice laid hold of the sodden blanket that was covering Ted Allan, and yanked. Water sloshed around his feet, three inches deep beneath the bunks. Allan lay shivering, his face white, a hand clasping his groin.

'Get on your feet,' Wales said roughly.

Allan looked at him, not seeming to focus; his eyes were strangely bright. He said, 'I don't feel too good.'

'None of us do. You must pull your weight, man! You're no first-voyager now. Come on—or Patience'll have your hide.'

Allan pulled himself to a sitting position. He shivered more than ever. 'Oh God, I can't. I really can't. It's my leg.'

'What about your leg?'

'It hurts a lot. High up—the thigh.'

With an impatience gesture Wales reached out and put a hand on the leg. Allan gave a sharp cry and sweat started on his forehead. 'Sorry,' Wales said. 'Get your trousers down and let's have a look.'

His face feverishly flushed now, Allan lifted his body from the bunk and eased his clothing away, helped by Wales. The senior apprentice looked and gave a whistle. 'It's swollen all right,' he said. 'What happened, Ted?'

'I got a frayed end of wire in it a

couple of days ago,' Allan said. 'Sliding down a backstay...didn't think too much of it at first, but now it's got really bad. I don't think I'll be much use on deck. I'm sorry.'

Wales put the clothing back in place and once again laid the blanket over. 'Just you stay put and don't worry. I'll tell Patience—and I'll get the peggy along to have a look.' The peggy was the steward, right-hand man of the Master on the medical side with a smattering of knowledge resting mainly upon aperients but capable of extension to bandages and poultices. Wales found him in his cabin aft.

'Allan's sick,' he said. 'Would you go along and take a look, while I report to the Mate?'

The steward, Vidler, wiped the back of a hand across his nose. 'What's up wiv 'im, then?'

Wales explained; then climbed to the poop where Patience was on watch. Patience blew up: he had plenty to say about young loafers but agreed that Allan could stay in his bunk until the steward had reported. This report was made within the next fifteen minutes and was made to

Mrs Landon in her husband's absence on deck—once again Landon was wearing ship in another attempt to catch that elusive shift of wind.

Vidler reported that young Allan had a leg full of poison. 'The lad's in a good deal of pain, I reckon, ma'am. Right thigh, come up the size of a balloon. I'll need to cut, likely.' Vidler coughed. 'I was wondering, like, if you'd kindly take a look, ma'am?'

Mary said at once, 'Of course I will.' She reached for an oilskin and sou'wester and followed the steward out. Vidler took her arm and steadied her along the reeling, slippery deck; they almost fell in through the door of the apprentices' accommodation. Ted Allan was holding fast to the sides of his bunk, his agony plain in his face, teeth held tight together. His skin was deeply flushed, the eyes feverish. Mary went to his side, smiling, laid cool hands on his forehead. 'You'll not mind if I take a look?'

'Oh, ma'am—'

'I shall have to nurse you, Ted, you must realize that.' She saw his embarrassment. 'Come along now.' Already she was removing the clothing. She was shocked at the evidence of poisoning but made no comment. 'We shall have to move you to the spare cabin aft. You'll be more comfortable there. Just leave it all to us. You'll be all right now, but it was very silly of you not to have spoken of this earlier.'

'I didn't want to put extra work on the others, ma'am.'

'That's all very well, but you must never neglect your own health, Ted. You'll be no use to anyone for a while now, until we've got rid of the poison, will you?' She smiled again, gently, ameliorating the rebuke. 'Keep still now and I'll see you're brought aft as soon as the men can be spared to carry you.'

She made her way carefully back to the saloon. She brought the copy of *The Ship Captain's Medical Guide* from the bookcase: this was the sole source of medical knowledge available aboard a ship at sea. Mary Landon had frequently assisted her husband in such matters, looking after the nursing of sick men, and on two occasions helping him in the appalling business of the amputation of a limb, carried out on the saloon table with the aid of a bottle of rum to deaden the pain. At first she had been intensely squeamish when entering an over-crowded fo'c'sle filled with semi-naked male bodies, but, largely because sailormen had a basic decency and a respect for women in such a situation, she had overcome her distaste and had found satisfaction in doing what she could for sick men, and had been touched by their gratitude.

Mary was still studying the medical guide when Landon came down from the poop. She reported the facts. Landon nodded, went back to the poop and had a word with Patience. Hands were detailed to carry Allan aft. Landon said, 'Mr Patience, when the time comes I'll need Chardonnet on the wheel. You'll kindly see to that.'

Patience, weary and ill-tempered, snapped, 'You and that Frenchy!'

'I beg your pardon, Mr Patience?'

Patience shrugged. 'Oh—nothing.'

Landon gave him a cold stare. 'It had better be—and you'll obey my orders without comment, Mister.' He turned away; if he should need to lance the thigh, he'd want the ship as steady as she could be held, and Chardonnet was the man for that.

The simple arrangements had been prepared by Vidler: two clean blankets in the spare cabin and a jug of steaming hot water in the tip-up washing cabinet. The primitive surgical instruments were laid out handy. When Ted Allan was brought aft, carried by Wales and Tom Chatto with the bosun standing by, Landon said, 'I'll examine him now.' He gestured the two apprentices out of the cabin and spoke in a low voice. 'By the sound of it, I may need some assistance shortly. How would you two youngsters feel about helping?'

Wales caught Tom's eye. 'We'd like to, sir.'

'Good—thank you. You know what I'm asking of you, Wales?'

Wales met the Master's eye. 'Hold him down, sir.'

Landon nodded. 'Neither easy nor pleasant, but part of your experience that may be useful one day.' He steadied himself against the heave and lurch of the ship as a sea passed beneath her counter. From the deck they heard the shouting voices of Patience and Underwood, and as the thump of blocks sounded from overhead Landon went back into the

221

cabin and stripped the blankets off his patient. Allan had a very high colour and his breathing was shallow; he was muttering more or less incoherently, unable to respond to questions. He was slipping fast into delirium, a rapid change, Landon thought, from his condition as reported by Mary. There was a convulsive heave and a gasp from the apprentice as Landon gently felt the exposed thigh. The flesh was badly distended, hard and hot to the touch. The area of inflammation was close to the groin—too close. If that should extend, the poison would creep into the trunk. Clearly, the time for poultices was well past.

'Damned young idiot,' Landon growled to his wife, who was beside him now. 'Will they never learn?' He shook his head sadly. 'You realize the dilemma, my dear?'

She said, 'You must lance, Theodore. I see no dilemma.'

'Do you not? I'm wondering if I should amputate, not merely cut the skin! It's a question of his life.'

She caught her breath at that. 'And his career on the other hand. To lose a leg—' She broke off. 'To be forced to leave the sea, to walk the rest of his days with a stump of wood? Oh, no, Theodore, not that.'

'You've seen it happen before.'

'Yes. But not to a boy.'

'It's better than death,' he said harshly. 'With God's help, I shall decide for the best.'

Landon bent again to examine the swollen, fiery flesh. Watching his face, Mary saw his lips moving and knew he was praying. So many times had she watched Theodore's face in the many moments of vital decision that came to a shipmaster, came almost daily in one form or another. Often she had wondered how any man could stand the mental strain, how he could go on taking the accusing faces when a wrong decision had been made, as was inevitable on occasion. No man was infallible, though it was always expected of a shipmaster that he should be... After a full minute had ticked away Landon gave a slight nod, then straightened and faced his wife.

'I shall lance,' he said. 'There is an inch or so to go before the trunk will be affected—I think it's a fair risk. Amputation will be a last resort.' He paused. 'Vidler?'

The steward was behind him. 'Yes, sir?'

'Start with the rum now. Chatto, my compliments to Mr Patience. Chardonnet is to take over the wheel at once, and remain there until further orders. The ship is to be held as steady as may be. Mr Patience is to have all hands standing by the braces. Hurry, now.'

Tom went off. When he returned to the cabin Vidler was holding the rum bottle to Allan's lips. A good deal of the spirit was being spilled. Mary Landon beckoned Wales and Tom towards the bunk. The patient was to be carried to the saloon table, where the overhead lamp gave more light. The two apprentices lifted their messmate, and with Vidler still holding the rum bottle to his lips, Allan was carried along the narrow alleyway into the saloon and laid on the table. There, Landon marshalled his helpers.

'Mary, take over the rum. Vidler, go to his head and hold the shoulders down—flat and square to the table. I'll want you, Wales on the right leg, Chatto on the left. Bear down smartly, and don't let go whatever happens.'

He turned to the surgical instruments and brought up a knife. He nodded at his wife and she laid down the rum, taking a sponge from the bowl of hot, soapy water. Gently she sponged the swollen flesh, then dried it with a clean towel. Jim Wales and Tom bore down hard on the legs at a word from Landon who then placed the tip of the knife against the distended skin after holding the blade for a moment in the flame of a candle lit by the steward.

Landon pressed with the knife-point.

The flesh dipped; there was a sharp cry from Allan and a convulsive jerk. Tom set his teeth hard, feeling the sweat break out on his body. As the knife went on pressing the flesh seemed to peel away from the blade and pus-stained blood welled out briefly in the instant before the dam broke. Allan's body writhed and the apprentices had their work cut out to hold the legs down. Landon laid the knife aside and pressed firmly on the flesh around the incision, his hands swathed in a clean linen cloth. Gout after gout of yellow pus was discharged: Allan must indeed, Tom thought, have been in agony.

'There's no more to come for now,' Landon said after a couple of minutes' squeezing. 'We must hope we've saved the leg.'

That evening Ted Allan was already better; the flush had gone from his face and though he was physically weak he had come out of his delirium. He told Tom that Captain Landon had said he needn't worry about losing his leg; the wound looked healthy now, though it would need regular attention for many days yet. Mary Landon and Vidler would see to that. Allan was immensely grateful for what had been done.

'Sorry to be a passenger,' he said, 'off Cape Stiff of all places...' His voice, as weak as his body, trailed away.

'Don't worry about that,' Tom said. He got to his feet and went aft. It was his watch below and he needed his sleep badly; he was fuzzy-minded with tiredness and knew that there had been moments when he'd been on the verge of falling asleep on his feet. It was a miracle to him that the Master and mates were able to keep awake during their everlasting pacing of the poop. He'd seen what an effort it was at times for Underwood to keep his eyes open, the lids constantly dropping as if weighted with lead and his gait like that of a drunk as he staggered and lurched up and down. The effort of keeping going was one of sheer will-power.

As Tom emerged from the saloon alleyway onto the open deck he all but cannoned into Chardonnet, who was descending the poop ladder. With one hand grasping the lifeline leading for'ard, Chardonnet asked in his improving English, 'How is the young boy?'

'A lot better, thank you—'

'*C'est bon.* I am glad.' He hesitated. '*M'sieur le capitaine...* he is a good doctor I think. No doubt *madame* is a good nurse, yes?'

'Yes—'

'She is attending him now?'

'Not just now,' Tom said.

'But soon, perhaps?'

'Perhaps. I don't know.'

'You can perhaps find out, and then tell me?'

There had been a curious insistence in the Frenchman's tone, in his manner too. Tom was cautious. 'Why do you ask?'

Chardonnet shrugged; in the fading light Tom saw a gleam of humour in the eyes. 'She is a woman, *mon garçon!* I am a man. That is all.'

Tom was frankly astonished. He said, 'In

a French ship...would a deckhand speak of the Captain's wife like that?'

Chardonnet laughed. 'To speak, this is nothing. In it is no sin, nor disrespect, nor insubordination. You are very young, *mon garçon.* But perhaps I should tell you—' He broke off as a shout came from the poop.

Patience was at the rail; he waved a fist. 'Get for'ard, you French bastard!' he yelled against the wind. 'Get you about your work—there's no time for yapping aboard a British ship. You too, Chatto. When you're off watch, you turn in.'

Chardonnet gestured with his fingers and seemed about to shout back at the Mate, but thought better of it and turned away with a shrug, making his way for'ard through the swirling water that was rising above the washports on the lee side. Tom went into the half-deck, out of the bitter weather into a cold, damp fug where at least the bulkheads gave protection against the flying ice slivers and the flurries of snow that blotted out the topmasts. Horatio Mainprice was lying on his bunk, fully dressed and shivering, with a scowl on his face. Tom grinned at him. 'Enjoying life?' he asked.

'Oh, shut up.'

'You sound as though you've had enough of the sea life.'

'You're not far wrong.' Suddenly Horatio gave a somewhat girlish giggle. 'Remember what that old blighter in the Line's offices said? Mr Ralph... "A man is a man and not an animal. The women of the ports are prowling beasts of prey." He says that to everyone. Ruddy old idiot! Me—I can't wait to get to Sydney and find out. Or Valparaiso at a pinch. What about you?'

Tom laughed. 'I suppose you're what Mr Ralph would call an animal.'

'Needs must,' Horatio said airily.

Tom shrugged. Mainprice said nothing further. A little later Tom went along to the galley for the apprentices' supper: the usual hash-up of dinner-time left-overs—crushed hard tack with a few fragments of salt horse. It was cold and nasty but when Tom had taken it back to the half-deck he ate gratefully if not with relish, then turned in. At a little before eight bells a man came in to wake Horatio for his watch, and the racket of this woke Tom as well. He saw dimly that the man was Chardonnet. He drifted off to sleep again, to be roughly woken a few minutes later, by which time Horatio had left the half-deck and Jim Wales had not yet come down. Lifting himself on one elbow, Tom asked, 'What is it now?'

Once again it was Chardonnet. The Frenchman's face was close to his. 'I have come to ask you to help me, *m'sieur.'*

'Help you? How?'

'I wish to talk to Madame Landon. If *you* ask, she will agree.'

'Why me?' Tom was bewildered.

'When you are with her,' Chardonnet said, 'I see that she is trustful of you. She will listen, as she would not listen to other persons.'

'You mean I'm the greenest, don't you?' Tom was worried now. His heart began to thump. 'You know it wouldn't be any good approaching anyone else, so—'

'Whatever the reason you will do as I say.' A threat had now come into Chardonnet's voice. 'Or it will be the worse for you.' Suddenly Tom felt a movement against his blankets and across his chest, and the next moment two sinewy hands met around his throat and gave a gentle squeeze. He gasped, and the hands tightened so that the gasp became a gurgle. Chardonnet said softly, 'That is what will happen, on deck one night when there is no moon...so you will speak to *madame* tomorrow, and to no one else, for if you do, be sure that I will know.'


## CHAPTER 12

When Tom was called for his watch he'd had little sleep. Wearily he stumbled out into the never-ending gale and reported to the poop where Underwood was taking over the deck. All hands of the watch, Tom included, were kept hard at it, tending the braces continually. Towards the end of the watch the sky began to lighten to a dismal grey and Tom looked out across the long, foam-capped waves that currently filled his world to the close horizons. It was a world of leaden desolation that affected the spirit; he felt they would never haul through again to the sun-filled skies.

In such grim surroundings the Frenchman's recent threat loomed larger than it might have done at other times, and Tom was quite unable to decide on a course of action. He was convinced that Chardonnet had no intention of letting the matter rest and he didn't know who to turn to. His duty would be to report the affair to the Master or the First Mate, but he shrank from this on account of the possible repercussions on Mary Landon. A sailing ship at sea was a small, closed world and tragic harm might well come of any clodhopping feet. Tom's notions were ill-formed and, like so many others, he had a basic mistrust of the French; thus with a Frenchman involved he could think no farther than some kind of clandestine love affair, an avenue of thought along which he had in any case been directed by Chardonnet's own words on deck before the man had approached him in the night. Certainly it had been deducible that Mary Landon was unwilling to give Chardonnet the opportunity for speech, but it was part of Tom's understanding that women were always contrary creatures...

He had almost made up his mind to take Jim Wales into his confidence when something happened that drove all thoughts of Chardonnet from his head. There was a roar from Underwood on the heaving, slippery poop:

'We have the shift...we have the shift of wind!'

At once the order was passed for All Hands. Underwood, after calling down the companion to rouse out the Master, began giving the orders that would bring the ship before the wind, which, with the curious suddenness that was a feature of any Cape Horn passage, had backed to the south-east. As it happened the *Pass of Drumochter* had been for a while on a northerly course away from the ice and up towards the Horn, and was currently on the port tack as she cut across the westerlies; thus the alteration needed was little enough. By the time Landon had reached the poop, still struggling into his oilskin, the ship was flying before the wind, heading north-westwards. She was breasting the rolling greybeards, rising to the crests, plunging over them to swoop like a bird down into the troughs, to lose the wind temporarily and then pick it up again as the waves flowed away astern and the bows lifted to the next breaker.

Landon, happier than for weeks past, shouted across the poop to the second Mate. 'Well done, Mr Underwood, well done indeed. Our position, if you please.'

'By dead reckoning, sir, almost due south of the Horn, a little under two hundred miles distant.'

Landon nodded. He had been studying the set of the sails, his big, bearded chin lifted, eyes narrowed against the blinding spray. 'With luck, the shift'll last long enough to carry us round without a sight of the Horn itself—but it may be only a fluke.' He looked around; Patience had now come up on deck, knuckling sleep from his eyes. 'Good morning, Mr Patience. We must not depend too much...we must take the fullest advantage while we can. So we'll get more canvas on her.' He rubbed his hands together briskly.

'A further shift might catch us unawares, Captain—'

'We must now allow it to catch us unawares, Mr Patience. She can carry a good deal more canvas than she has on her now. You'll shake out all sail to the upper tops'ls on the fore and main—and be quick about it.' Landon made another critical examination of sea and sky and added, 'She'll stand t'gallants'ls as well—fore and main both. See to it, Mr Patience.'

Patience began to argue. 'I don't reckon—'

'You heard my order, Mister. See to it—at once. Get the hands aloft.'

Patience shrugged, turned away surlily, and began bellowing at the men. Already standing by expectantly, they swarmed up the ratlines to lie out along the yards, feet slipping and sliding on the ice-covered footropes. Letting go the frozen bunts and gaskets with fumbling fingers equally frozen they beat out the sails, hammering with bleeding fists at the canvas that was as hard and unyielding as a board, while the ship rose and plunged again and again beneath them with a shrieking wind ripping through the spider's-web of ropes and spars. O'Connor was aloft with the fo'c'sle gang; and all the apprentices except Ted Allan, still on the sick list in the spare cabin, were also taking a full part. Tom was on the fore upper topsail yard when he found Chardonnet working alongside him; there were in fact just the two of them on the weather side. Close to Tom's ear the Frenchman asked, 'You have done as I said, *m'sieur?*'

'Not...yet.'

'But you are going to.'

'I don't know.' Tom's flesh crawled; he was in a bad position for an argument, almost eighty feet above the turbulence of the icy seas. He saw the hard anger in the Frenchman's face, the ugly glint in the dark eyes, and felt the tension in the man's sinews as the lithe body pressed close to his own. Chardonnet said, 'You are being troublesome, *mon garçon.* This I do not like. Remember what I said. Look down, *m'sieur*—look down at the deck, and at the water.'

Involuntarily Tom did so. Chardonnet laughed. 'One push and you are dead. The deck will break your back, or the sea will freeze you instantly. But it is not necessary—it is not much I ask of you. Think well, *garçon.* There will be other times when we shall be up here, alone together.'

He stayed close. Like Tom's, his breath was freezing as he exhaled; Tom could feel the thin crackle of the ice-web as it met his cheek. A little more pressure next time from that supple body and a quick final shove, and his feet would slide from the footrope; it would take no more than a tap on his frozen fingers to release his grip on the yard and that would be that. And no-one any the wiser. The enquiry into his death would be perfunctory: few ships made the east-west passage of the Horn without an accident, genuine or otherwise, and nobody thought anything of it. Chardonnet would keep his nose clean; there would be no proof.

'Well, *m'sieur?*'

Tom temporized. 'If you'd tell me what you want with Mrs Landon...'

Again Chardonnet laughed; he seemed about to say something further when there was a shout from the deck far below and the Frenchman looked down briefly. 'We must work,' he said. 'The Mate, he watches. Come now.' He began beating again at the rigid canvas. Working with grim determination, balanced on their bellies across the yard, they freed the sail and then the men on deck tailed onto the ropes and the sail was hauled out on the lifts. 'Now we go down,' Chardonnet said. 'But first another word.' He paused. 'While working, I have thought. I shall tell you what I want with *madame.'* He was moving inwards now, towards the mast. Tom was following. Chardonnet went on as they reached the shrouds, 'I want only information. That is all.'

'What sort of information?'

'I wish to know what are the intentions

237

of *m'sieur le capitaine*... as to myself.' With one hand grasping the shrouds, Chardonnet turned to look full at Tom. 'Is it his intention to hand me over in Valparaiso, or in Sydney, or perhaps to take me back to England?'

'I've no idea,' Tom said blankly.

'Of course you have not, *m'sieur,* but I think *madame* will be able to discover this, no?'

Reluctantly Tom nodded. 'Yes, I suppose so.'

'Good. Then you will ask her, and you will tell me.' Chardonnet slid his hand into his waistband and partially withdrew a small knife. 'You understand, do you not?'

Tom swallowed. 'If I do as you ask...then you'll not need to speak yourself to Mrs Landon?'

'No. I think you will tell me the truth of what I wish to know. But remember this: *m'sieur le capitaine* is not to know that I have asked for the information. This you will tell *madame.'*

'Why? In fact, if that's all you want to know, why not ask the Captain yourself?' He added, 'Surely it'd be natural enough, for you to want to know?'

Not meeting Tom's eye Chardonnet said, 'If I should show too much curiosity, then I believe *le capitaine* would not tell me the truth, in case I should break for the shore at some port before he could hand me over.'

It wasn't an entirely satisfactory answer but there was no time for further questions. Already Chardonnet was on his way down; and the moment he reached the deck he was roped in by the bosun to lend a hand at the main yard. At the same time Patience yelled out for Tom to make all speed for the weather main brace and for the rest of the time until one watch was sent below Tom and Chardonnet were kept busy and separated. Tom, however, went on worrying. Chardonnet's explanation had sounded plausible up to a point but Tom was convinced there was something more behind it. In any event he thought it highly unlikely that Chardonnet would be given any chance to break for the shore. Patience, let alone the Old Man, would see to that.

That night the *Pass of Drumochter*, still well to the south, made the passage of the Horn into the Pacific Ocean without ever once bringing the Cape itself into view; and once he had made enough westing Landon brought her round to the north to head up towards the west coast of South America for Valparaiso in Chile. Once again, in the foul weather conditions that still persisted in the high south latitudes, it was a case of All Hands; and when the watch below was at last dismissed to turn in, leaving the deck watch to tack the ship up across the westerlies, Tom found himself alone in the half-deck with Jim Wales.

As Wales dropped thankfully into his bunk Tom said, indeed almost blurted out, 'You told me once, I could come to you for advice.'

Wales sighed. 'Yes, I did. Can't it wait till morning?'

Tom looked dashed but reached up with the intention of dowsing the hanging oil-lamp. 'I suppose it can, yes.'

Wales sat up. 'Wait a minute, kid. If it's really bothering you I'll listen. What's the trouble?'

Tom told him. When he had finished he said, 'I just don't know what to do. If I make a report to Patience or the Old Man, Chardonnet's going to find out sooner or later.'

'Yes, he probably would,' Wales agreed. 'D'you reckon he means what he said, about that threat to do you in?'

'Yes.'

'You sound pretty sure.'

'I am.'

Wales gave him a shrewdly appraising look. Rubbing his chin he reflected that murder was easily enough done at sea; if it happened now it wouldn't be the first time by any means, nor the last. He said, 'All the secrecy...it could be he means to go overboard somewhere off the coast and try to make it ashore. That is, if the Old Man's decided to hand him over in Valparaiso.'

'It'd be a big risk.'

'A man in the Frenchy's position needs to set one risk against another, Tom. If you're thinking of sharks, well, I don't think the risk's too great down this way. Besides, Landon has a reputation for sailing close to the shore once he's around the Horn—close to the offshore islands, that is. The Frenchy'll have heard that, I dare say, from the hands. I'd wager that's what he means to do, right enough.'

'And then what? What happens to him after that?'

With a laugh Wales said, 'That's not for us to worry about, is it? He'll maybe find work ashore...one thing's certain, and that is, he's not likely to be picked up again.' He pondered, eyes screwed up in thought. 'If I were you, Tom, I'd do just as Chardonnet asks. Look at it this way: I'm not sure you can blame any fo'c'sle hand for deserting. It's a pretty hellish life for the poor sods—you've seen that for yourself by now. If the Frenchy gets away, none of us is going to be any the worse off. I'd be inclined to say good luck to him, kid.'

'But wouldn't—'

'Look,' Wales said, 'it's late, or early depending which way you see it, and I'm too damn whacked to think straight. We'll talk about it in the morning, all right?'

'All right,' Tom said miserably. He reached up and dowsed the lamp, then climbed into his bunk and tried to sleep amid the oily stench from the lamp's lingering fumes and the nightmare of his own thoughts. He hated to admit it even to himself, but he was thoroughly afraid of the Frenchman and had no doubts at all that the threat to his own life was real.

The solution offered by Wales would at least have the merit of saving his own skin. Yet how could he remain silent? All the while he was remembering those words spoken to him by Mary Landon, so long ago it seemed now, the words that she had bitten off too late: '*A man who has killed once—*' And he was recalling, too, his own promise to her that he would never say a word to anyone else. But how could he connive at the escape of a murderer? and would not Landon be liable to face a charge of compounding a felony, of being an accessory or however the law might phrase it?

Wales didn't know about any of that: Tom's promise to Mary Landon had held.

When Tom was roused out next morning for his watch Wales was still asleep; and when his watch was over Tom went aft to the spare cabin where Ted Allan was still berthed.

They talked, Tom lingering as long as he could in the hope that Landon's wife would come in. And after he'd been there for some ten minutes, she did. When she left, Tom followed her out into the alleyway. Keeping his voice low he said,

'Ma'am, there's something I must speak to you about.'

'Yes, Tom?'

'Privately, if you please, ma'am.'

She looked at him closely and he detected alarm. He said, 'It's about Chardonnet, ma'am.'

'I see.' A hand went to her breast. 'Come to the saloon. My husband's on deck.' She led the way to the saloon, where she turned to face him. He told her as briefly as possible of his conversations with Chardonnet. 'I think perhaps he means to get away by jumping overboard whilst we head up the coast, ma'am. Do you know what the Captain intends to do with him?'

She shook her head. 'My husband has not spoken of that to me—I doubt if he's decided yet. But this threat to you, Tom...do you believe Chardonnet is serious?'

'I do, ma'am! That's why I ask that nothing should become known to anyone that I've—'

'It won't be,' she said at once. 'I promise you that, Tom.'

'Except that I think you must tell the Captain.'

'Yes...'

'And I shall go back to Chardonnet, and tell him I've found out the Captain hasn't yet decided what to do?' He looked at her questioningly.

She nodded. 'Yes, Tom, do that. And—thank you for telling me.'

'That's all right, ma'am,' he said awkwardly. He left the saloon and went back on deck. As he went out through the door from the alleyway he glanced back and saw Mary Landon standing outside the saloon, staring after him with a faraway look in her eyes as if she was not seeing him at all.

On deck it was still bitterly cold, still overcast; the sea was still being nipped off in spray by a strong wind, but there was some lightening of the atmosphere and a feeling now of hope that they were coming clearer each minute of the desolation of Cape Horn, that they were moving up into the sun and warmth of easier waters. As he made for the half-deck Tom became aware of someone behind him and, turning, he came face to face with Chardonnet.

'You have done what I said, no?'

'Yes—'

'You were a long time, *m'sieur?*'

'You saw me go in?'

Chardonnet grinned. 'But yes, *m'sieur.*'

Tom explained that he'd been visiting Ted Allan. 'I had to wait till I could catch Mrs Landon alone.'

'And the answer?'

Tom said steadily, 'The Captain hasn't decided yet. Or if he has, he's said nothing to Mrs Landon.'

Chardonnet's face darkened. 'You are telling me the truth? If you are—'

'It's the truth.' In spite of the cold, Tom felt a clammy sweat break out.

Chardonnet nodded. 'Very well. *Madame* will press *m'sieur* to decide?'

'Yes, she will.'

'And then you will find out, and you will tell me. Very well—I shall be patient. But not for too long. Never forget what I said.' Chardonnet moved away along the deck, making for the fo'c'sle, and Tom went into the half-deck where he found that Horatio Mainprice had brought the dinner from the galley: dandy funk, a compound of the usual powdered biscuit with water and molasses. It was the first really warm meal for a long while.

'It's no more than the boy's word,' Landon said gruffly.

'The lad would never lie, Theodore.'

'I didn't mean to imply that. But he's very young—a first-voyager, and impressionable. Besides, I have his story only at second hand. I shall need to talk to the boy himself, Mary, then I shall see what must be done.'

'Yes, Theodore,' she said meekly. Even captains' wives didn't go overtly against the Master; but there were ways. Looking at Landon speculatively she asked, 'How often do you speak to the apprentices alone, Theodore?'

He pursed his lips. 'Seldom—seldom. Yes...I think I see what you mean.'

She underlined it. 'In the circumstances it wouldn't be long before Chardonnet got to hear about your speaking to the boy in private, and then—'

'Yes. There is a risk. You seem very sure the boy will come to harm.'

'I believe what he said. And I think he showed a great deal of courage in speaking to me at all.'

'He knows where his duty lies. I find that pleasing at all events.'

She said with a smile, 'Jodurecom?'

'Jodurecom, yes.' Landon paced the saloon, back and forth, powerful hands clasped beneath the tails of his unbuttoned coat. 'Obviously the boy cannot be placed in danger of such a sort, but equally obviously I cannot order all members of my crew to keep a watch on Chardonnet. Oh, I know well enough what you think I should do, Mary.' He stopped his pacing and turned to face his wife, a hand tugging at his beard. 'Nevertheless, I'm most reluctant to have the man, let's say, confined to the fore peak on the unsupported word of an impressionable lad...especially after Chardonnet has given excellent service all along—why, he's the best helmsman I have by far!'

'Theodore—'

'Consider, my dear: there would be no reason I could give to the men—other than to admit the facts, and it has been my hope all the time that nothing of the man's past would emerge until after he has left the ship. Nor could I allow rumours to circulate. The moment I confined Chardonnet below, there could well be trouble. No, Mary, I shall not have him locked up. Besides, without him we would be two men short, with young Allan still sick—quite apart from the loss of Lacey and Ballantyne north of the Equator. Four short is—'

'Allan will be fit to work by tomorrow,' she told him. 'I've kept him in bed as a precaution, that's all. Well, Theodore? It's not for me to say, but I do think this is a matter that *must* be decided quickly. You must not forget what we know about Chardonnet.'

'Ha! I'm scarcely likely to do that.' Landon tugged again at his beard, obviously troubled, then swung away with a sudden movement. 'I must have a little more time to think, Mary. I do not believe that Chardonnet would let me down to the extent you are suggesting.'

'Well, you must have your think, Theodore—I shall say no more.'

Landon murmured something about keeping a weather eye lifted on Chardonnet and young Chatto, and seeing things for himself, then stumped out of the saloon, going up the companion to the poop. Mary listened to his heavy footsteps on the deck above; she sighed and picked up some sewing. She had done what she could. There was a point beyond which her husband would not tolerate female interference and he could become exceedingly obstinate if pressed. He was already being obstinate and in Mary's view he had not quite the insight into men's characters, despite his years of command, that he believed himself to have. He tended too much to see the best in people, possibly because of his own innate decency.

From that time onward Landon spent most of his time on deck, sometimes accompanied by his wife, sometimes pacing the poop alone with his thoughts. All the time he was keeping that weather eye lifted on his crew, watching Chardonnet when the man was at the wheel or working aloft or about the decks, watching Tom Chatto as well; being especially watchful when the two were in each other's company.

He saw nothing to give him any clues or any cause for anxiety and gradually his fears subsided. He was still most reluctant to confine Chardonnet below but knew that he must put the man ashore at Valparaiso and face up himself to the consequences of having concealed him at Recife. All he could do would be to make an honest statement and trust himself to the mercies of the British consul. Although he, Landon, had never indulged in any kind of knavery in his life, it was a widely accepted fact that there were plenty of shipmasters who would use literally any means of getting together a full crew to take their ships around Cape Horn and this the consul would know very well.

The *Pass of Drumochter* continued on passage northwards without incident, sailing up past the cluttered inlets and offshore islands that festooned the southern coast of Chile. The Strait of Magellan, Desolation Island, the Queen Adelaide Archipelago...up towards Hanover Island and Madre de Dios and on to Campana Island. The weather lightened almost hourly; cold it still was, but the sun shone again and damp clothes dried out for the first time in weeks. Spirits improved miraculously as the men's bodies thawed and the food was served hot and Landon ordered more canvas broken out from the yards. The *Pass of Drumochter* bowled along with all sail set to the royals and skysails, with a fair wind bellying out the canvas and putting a bone in her teeth as she cut through the South Pacific.

Towards evening as some days later his ship came up to Cerro San Valentin, standing not so far off the outer islands in accordance with his custom—it gave the men heart, Landon believed, to see land after weeks of battling through lonely seascapes—Landon had a word with Tom Chatto, who was overhauling the pendant of the spanker boom, the very piece of gear that had almost caused his wife's death. Watching the boy, Landon had seen with approval that he was shaping into a good seaman, deft with his hands, nimble on his feet, and with a good intelligence that could already anticipate an order.

Now, Landon stood looking down at him. 'How did you like the Horn?' he asked.

Tom got to his feet politely. 'I didn't, sir. It was rotten all the way, sir.' Tom spoke with feeling.

Landon laughed. 'That's honest enough! I appreciate honesty. Remain honest, boy—and never be discouraged by Cape Horn. You'll see it often enough, and curse it often enough too, so long as you stay with the Line, but remember it's but a part of a long and rewarding passage. No more than that.'

'Yes, sir.'

'None of us likes the Horn, you never

grow really used to it but it's there and has to be rounded.' Landon paused; they were talking naturally enough and the Second Mate, who had the watch, was by the rail passing down orders to the hands on deck. Master and junior apprentice were as alone as they would ever be short of a too pointed summons to the saloon. Speaking quietly Landon said, 'Carry on working, Chatto, and listen to me. Mrs Landon has spoken to me. Do you understand me?'

Tom nodded. 'Yes, sir.'

'Now tell me honestly: has Chardonnet been troubling you?'

Tom hesitated for a moment; he'd been surprised to find that the Frenchman had laid doggo. 'No, sir. Not since I spoke to Mrs Landon.'

Landon felt much relieved. 'Do you believe his intentions are still as you thought?'

'I don't know, sir. He—he may have had further thoughts, sir.'

'Yes. Very well, boy. That's all I have to ask.'

Going down the companion a few minutes later, Landon found his mind more at rest. Chatto had by no means given any indication of fear and Landon had never wholly believed Chardonnet would harm a youngster. Women, even dearly loved wives, were seldom good interpreters, being far too emotional and unpredictable...

At midnight Tom was asleep in the half-deck, as was Ted Allan, now returned to duty and hard living with a thick bandage around his thigh. Wales had come down from his watch on relief by Horatio Mainprice and was turning in. Underwood was taking over the poop from the Mate; and the remainder of the new watch were turning out from the fo'c'sle, sleepily grousing at a sailor's lot. They settled down to their various duties; there was in fact little to do other than watch the sails and hold themselves ready to trim the yards if so ordered by the Second Mate. The ship ran on with a degree of relaxed sleepiness that would never have been possible farther south; all hands were taking things more or less easily and in any event Mr Underwood, unlike Mr Patience, was never a driver.

At four bells Paul Chardonnet took over for his trick at the wheel and soon after this Underwood, yawning and heavy-eyed, drifted to the fore end of the poop and draped his body, arms folded comfortably, over the rail and let his thoughts drift to a girl in far-off Liverpool Town. Horatio Mainprice had been sent for'ard to check on the anchor strops. Away to starboard ran the long line of the Chilean coast and it's off-shore islands. The binnacle lamp flickered across the Frenchman's face, which was without expression as his fingers gave the wheel a slight starboard bias, watching as he did so the weather leech of the main topgallant-sail—which was where the Second Mate's attention should also have been. As Chardonnet moved the wheel cautiously there was in fact no noticeable change in the rhythm of the rippling movement of the leech. He moved the wheel over further.

It was a little before five bells that the apprentices in the half-deck, and the officers aft, were brought to sudden and painful wakefulness on being thrown violently from their bunks by a tremendous concussion.

They came out on deck to hear cries from the fo'c'sle as water gushed aft from the broken door. Fragmented woodwork was carried along on the flood. The ship, motionless now, was up by the head, her bows lifted at an angle of some twenty degrees to the fore-and-aft line. On the poop, Underwood was lying flat, and blood was running sluggishly across the deck planking from a deep gash in his back; and as Landon came pounding up from the cabin below a heavy boot took him full in the face. As he went crashing back down the companion ladder, Chardonnet ran across the poop and jumped from the starboard rail into the shallows.

## CHAPTER 13

It was Patience who found the Captain being tended by his wife, and lying at the foot of the ladder, Patience who had rushed through the saloon shouting oaths, with a shoulder painful from his sudden projection out of his bunk. Landon's face was deathly white and bleeding and he seemed to be struggling round from unconsciousness.

'What happened?' Patience demanded.

Landon shook his head. His voice was weak. 'Get on deck, Mr Patience...the Frenchman...'

'The bloody Frenchy!'

'Lose no time.' Landon's words came out with an effort. 'I believe...Chardonnet...has put my ship aground...'

'The devil he has.' Patience stared at the Captain for a moment then collected himself and moved fast. He leapt over Landon's form and made for the ladder. He found fearful confusion on deck, men running here and there without apparent purpose, saw the water swilling through from the fo'c'sle door. Wales was coming aft followed by the other apprentices. Patience shouted, 'Which of you lads was on watch?'

'Me, sir—'

'Mainprice, eh. What happened, boy?'

'We hit for'ard, sir—'

'I've gathered that much! Where's Chardonnet?' The Mate, moving to the rail, saw Underwood lying on the deck. 'My God,' he said, and bent. 'Chris...are you all right?'

There was no answer. Patience straightened Underwood's body, saw the staring eyes, the slackly open mouth, the blood on the deck. The Second Mate was clearly dead. Patience turned the body over: death had been caused by a knife-thrust in the back.

Patience said, 'Well, Mainprice? *What about Chardonnet?*'

Horatio was staring down at the body, his face twitching. 'I—I can't say, sir. I was for'ard when the ship hit. I didn't see Chardonnet.'

'For'ard, were you?'

'Yes, sir. Mr Underwood had sent—'

'Did you see anything ahead—any reefs, any rocks?'

Horatio shook his head. 'No, sir. Nothing, before or after.'

'Then we've hit a submerged rock. And the Frenchy's gone more than likely.' There was an odd intensity in the Mate's voice that scared Horatio. 'Get you down to the cabin, boy. You'll find the Captain injured...ask him, from me, for the key of the safe where he keeps his pistol. Bring the pistol up to me here—and be quick about it!'

'Aye, aye, sir.' Horatio turned and ran for the companion. Patience shouted for'ard: 'Bosun, lay aft, at the double!'

'Here, sir,' a voice said. O'Connor was already coming up the ladder from the waist.

'What's the state of the ship, O'Connor?'

'No immediate danger, sir. Transverse

bulkhead's holding. Carpenter's sounding round now.' O'Connor was breathing hard. 'The fo'c'sle's a bloody mess and the stores and fore peak are flooded, but no injuries to the hands so far as I've seen.'

Patience nodded; he told the bosun that Chardonnet was believed to have jumped ship after possibly putting her aground deliberately. He said, 'I'm going after him. While I'm gone, I want a search made of the ship just in case he's still aboard but I don't reckon he is and I'm not delaying while the search is carried out.' He wiped the back of a hand across his forehead; he was streaming sweat. 'I'll want four of the men, O'Connor, the younger ones—and you,' he added to Tom, 'can come with me as well. So can Mainprice.'

He turned to Jim Wales. 'As for you, you're nearly out of your time and I have a good opinion of you. So has Captain Landon, and I'm going to ask him to appoint you uncertificated Third Mate for the time being, acting Second in the room of Mr Underwood. You'll take command in my absence if the Captain should not be fit. You'll be guided in all matters by the carpenter and the bosun and you'll do your best between you to keep the ship afloat. All right, lad?'

Wales nodded. 'All right, sir.'

'Good. I'll be relying on you, so will the Captain.' Patience laid a hand briefly on his shoulder. As he turned away Horatio Mainprice came up from the cabin, holding Landon's pistol and a box of cartridges. He handed these to Patience. Patience said, 'I'm going below for a word with the Captain. I want the landing party ready and waiting when I come up. See to it, O'Connor—and have the lifeboat in the water aft.'

'Aye, sir.' The bosun clattered down the ladder. Aloft in the darkness the sails flapped dismally, slatting against the masts as they were stirred by a light wind. Tom found it an eerie sight to see the *Pass of Drumochter* so suddenly lifeless, so suddenly stopped in her tracks. He felt a sadness for the ship and for her Master, though this was overlaid by a surge of excitement at the thought of the forthcoming chase after the fugitive. Already now hands were aloft on the foremast, getting the headsails off her to help lighten her for'ard. When this had been done as a first priority, the remaining canvas would be sent down in case any increase in the wind should drive her harder against the rocks.

Three minutes later Patience was back on deck. 'The Captain's not too good,' he told Wales. 'Unconscious again. He took a nasty crack on the head when that French bastard knocked him down the ladder, and his right shoulder's injured too. He'll be all right with Mrs Landon and Vidler seeing to him, but for now, the ship's yours—Mister Wales.'

Wales looked momentarily surprised at being addressed as Mister before he remembered his new, if temporary, status. The First Mate's use of the term brought his sudden responsibilities home to him forcibly and he said, 'Then I'll be going about my work, sir.'

Patience nodded. He ran an eye over the landing party assembled by the bosun. 'Now, you'll all know what we have to do—find the Frenchy! That's all. We don't know where to look I'll admit, so all we can do is to get ashore at the nearest point and hope we can pick up a trail. One thing's sure—it's a wild coast around here. He'll find no help and he'll not be able to walk forever.'

'Nor will we,' Horatio Mainprice murmured.

Patience heard that. He rounded on the apprentice. 'Shut your mouth. And remember this, you bloody little Lord High Admiral—I'm taking you along only because you'd be no damn use to the ship if I left you. Understand?'

'Yes, sir—'

'But even you have one asset: your eyes. Use 'em. Use 'em all the way along. Don't let anything escape 'em or you'll have me and the Captain to answer to.'

When the lifeboat was in the water Patience embarked his landing party and with a man taking soundings with a hand line the boat was pulled ahead slowly towards the fore part of the ship where Patience took a critical look at the damage. The stem was fast, right enough, but it could have been worse; it should not be impossible to plug any leaks, effect makeshift repairs and kedge the ship free.

The boat's crew then pulled inshore, into a fiord-like bay, one of many that broke up the coast in deep indentations. They came onto a beach, silver beneath a bright moon; Patience sent the boat and its crew back at once, for all possible hands would be needed aboard and so would the boat itself.

Bringing out the Captain's pistol he said, 'So far so good. Now I want you to spread out along the shore at fifty-yard intervals and look for tracks. Sing out the moment you spot anything.'

By morning Patience was in a vile mood and all hands were feeling the lash of his bitter tongue. No progress had been made and the seamen were in a fair way to being lost themselves. Initially they had picked up some footprints on the sandy shore but these tracks had done no more than lead Patience towards the forest behind. There, not unnaturally, the trail had vanished and Patience, soon raw like the others from the bites of insects and the scrape of branches, had become flummoxed. He had no experience of navigating through trees and was as helpless as a Mid-Western cowhand would have been off the pitch of the Horn.

Nevertheless, by use of a hand compass to guide him in an easterly direction, the Mate had pushed on through the night, climbing, eventually, ground that rose steeply; and having looked at the chart of the area before leaving the ship, he knew that he was in the foothills of the Chilean Andes, though he knew little else; the chart had been less than specific about the landward section. When his turnip-shaped timepiece and a faint lightening of the blackness told him there should by now be daylight above the treetops, Mr Patience, cursing and scratching, called one more halt in the series of brief rests that had broken up the night's slog.

'It's no damn use,' he snapped. 'We haven't a dog's chance of finding him now. That Frenchy, damn his guts...he knew what he was doing.' He dropped to the ground, puffing and blowing; then, seeing something in the light of the flickering storm lantern that he was carrying, he leapt to his feet with an oath, dragged out the pistol, and fired. There was a sharp yelp from Horatio Mainprice; Patience told him to shut his face.

'What was it, sir?' Horatio asked in a squeaking voice.

Patience, searching with much caution, snapped, 'A damned serpent I could have sworn. I reckon I got him, but I can't be sure.'

'But sir—'

Patience, hissing as though he were himself a serpent, said, 'Well, Admiral Mainprice, what is it now?'

'I doubt if you'll find snakes here, sir. It's far too cold, I assure you.'

'When I want your expertise, boy, I'll ask for it.' Patience poked around a little longer, then gave it up. Tom made a suggestion.

'Would it help if we split up, sir?'

'No. Use some sense, Chatto. If we could split into a hundred bloody parts, it still wouldn't be enough to cover all this ground. And once we'd parted, we'd likely never come together again.' Patience drew the sleeve of his heavy pilot-cloth jacket across his face. He said viciously, 'By God, Landon's been asking for this! If I warned him once about that damned Frenchy, why, I must have done so a dozen times or more.'

Tom didn't comment. It was no use crying over spilt milk; and it was obvious to him that the chase was one of sheer revenge on the part of Mr Patience who was determined to get even. As the Mate went on grumbling Tom said, 'He can't last out here on his own, sir. He'll die. Wouldn't that be the best thing?'

'Are you teaching me my duty, Chatto? Are you?' The Mate thrust his face close; he looked dangerous and threatening. 'If so, you can shut your mouth, d'you hear me, or it'll be the worse for you when we get back aboard. I'll find that bastard if it takes a year.' Patience glowered, and his fists clenched, but after a few moments he subsided. He lowered his body back to the ground, and sat, despondently, with his head in his hands and his elbows resting on his thighs. He stared moodily ahead into the glimmerings of the dawn, eyes and expression blank. After a while he stirred himself to call out to one of the seamen to issue rations, and they breakfasted on a sip of water and two hard ship's biscuits per man. When the meagre ration had been consumed Tom risked another suggestion.

'Do you think it might be better if we headed north, sir, rather than continue east?'

Patience turned and stared. 'You're the clever little bugger, aren't you? Tell me why I should think that.'

'Well, sir, I think Chardonnet would go north. Even if he were able to cross the Andes to the east, there'd be very little civilization for a pretty long way, sir.'

'I see,' Patience said heavily. 'And where did you learn all that, might I ask?'

'In geography, sir. At school.'

'Really! Well, boy, if you ask me, I'd say the same would be the case going north.'

'Perhaps, sir,' Tom answered diplomatically. 'But surely the going would be easier, northward? There wouldn't be the mountain range to cross. Chardonnet would be likely to take the easier and faster route, wouldn't he, sir?'

Patience gave a disagreeable grunt but seemed to waver. 'Six of one, half a dozen of the other.' He was silent for a while. 'Yet there's a grain of sense maybe,' he said grudgingly, 'even though it comes from a green enough source. We'll try for the north, then.'

They got going again immediately, Patience finding his northerly course by compass and lantern. The going was as slow and heavy as before. The struggle was the worse because every man knew in his heart that the attempt was as near hopeless as to be impossible; and knew, too, as Tom had surmised, that they were being used in the Mate's personal vendetta.

Back aboard the *Pass of Drumochter* all hands had worked throughout the night and there was no respite as dawn broke over the water and the desolate Chilean coastline to starboard. Under the direction of the bosun and carpenter all inboard soundings had been taken and it had been confirmed to Jim Wales that the ship was not taking water anywhere except in the damaged part for'ard of the reinforced bulkhead. She had in fact touched only very lightly, striking, as the outboard soundings with the hand-lead had proved, a shelving section of submerged rock up which she had slid to rest; and the carpenter gave it as his opinion, when the ebbing tide exposed the whole stem, that it should be possible to make a running repair with planking and canvas and plenty of Stockholm tar, enough to keep the water from the fore part which could then be pumped out so that she would lift again by the head.

'Will we be able to sail her?' Wales asked.

Dabbs scratched his head. 'Maybe with just the maincourse on her to give steerage way through the water. Any more pressure than that, she might not take it, lad.' He grinned. 'Sorry—Mister.'

Wales nodded. 'How about getting her off, for a start?'

'Hang on till next high water after we've done the repair, then lay out kedge anchors with the lifeboat. Reckon that should do it—eh, bose?'

'It might at that,' O'Connor said. 'But if I were you, I'd not start coming off till Mr Patience is back aboard. I wouldn't feel too happy, drifting around off this here coast. Once we're off, we'll want to pull the head round and catch a wind that'll take us out to open water straight away—'

'And we can't do that till everyone's back aboard—of course not.' Wales told the carpenter to start his preparations for repair. 'I'll have a word with the Captain in the meantime.'

Dabbs asked, 'How's 'e coming along, Mister Wales?'

'He'll live! But he'll have to stay in his bunk for a while yet.'

Dabbs grinned. 'Mrs Landon's orders, eh?'

'That's right. He's old, to take that kind of thing.'

'You're telling me,' Dabbs said, spitting over the side. 'By god, if they bring that Frenchy back alive, I reckon he's in for a lynching! I'd like the personal pleasure of hoisting him to the main t'gallant yard to swing, so help me!' Wales saw that the carpenter's fists were clenched into tight, hard balls at his sides. 'Talking of which reminds me, Mister. How about Mr Underwood? Do we have him sewn up now, or not?'

'I'll have to ask the Captain,' Wales answered. He went aft to the poop. Going in through the saloon alleyway, he found the steward and asked if it would be possible to speak to the Captain.

'Not for too long,' Vidler warned. 'He's been in a fair old state about that Frenchy. I dessay 'e'll be glad enough of a word with you.'

'Mrs Landon?'

Vidler jerked a hand towards the cabin. 'In there with 'im.'

Wales carried on through the empty saloon and knocked at the Captain's door. Mary Landon called out, 'Come in.'

Wales was shocked at the sight of Landon, propped up in his bunk with two pillows. Overnight, he had become a very old man, white and strained, with red-rimmed staring eyes and an obvious inertia in his limbs. In a croaking voice he asked, 'Is there any word from the shore, Wales?'

'No, sir. The moment there is, I'll report to you, sir.'

Landon lifted a shaking hand to the bandages on his head and shoulder. 'I fear the results of this business, Wales.'

'I'd try not to worry, sir.' Jim Wales was embarrassed. He asked a stupid question. 'Are you comfortable, sir?'

Landon tried to laugh. 'Far from it, though my wife and Vidler between them have done everything possible.' The Captain looked at Mary fondly, and there was a mistiness in his eyes as though he were plagued with self-blame for bringing trouble into her life. 'Tell me—how is the ship?'

'Safe enough, sir. We can make repairs.' Wales told Landon in detail what Dabbs and O'Connor had reported. 'I've looked for myself, sir. We're in not too bad a way.' He paused. 'Have you any orders, sir?'

'Just that you should carry on, Wales. You must watch carefully for any hint of a real blow, and try to anticipate it. A heavy wind catching us...whilst on the rocks, we would be in danger of breaking up. You must keep me informed.'

'Of course, sir. Just now there's no wind to speak of, a lightbreeze from the sou'-west, scarcely enough to ruffle the water.'

Wearily Landon nodded. 'We're lucky, Wales, lucky. God is with us. I trust He will guide Mr Patience aright also.'

'Yes, sir,' Wales said awkwardly. He broached the subject of Underwood's disposal: Landon's answer was as he'd expected—the body must be preserved at least until the ship had come off the rocks. Once in deep water a sea committal might take place but on the other hand it might be necessary to carry it on to Valparaiso as evidence. Landon was obviously tiring and did not wish to come to an immediate decision; and Wales, catching Mary Landon's eye, saw the almost imperceptible nod towards the door. He took the hint, saying, 'I'll be about my duties, sir,' and turned away from the bunk. Mary came out with him, closing the door gently behind her.

'How is he really, ma'am?' Wales asked.

She hesitated. 'Well—he's no longer young Jim. The kick was a brutal one, and the fall down the ladder shook him very badly. And of course the—the murder. But it's largely his anxiety too,' she added, and there was a good deal of anxiety in her own face as she said it.

'Chardonnet, ma'am?'

'Yes. If he has to report that he's let a known deserter who's committed murder get away, that he—' She broke off, swaying back against the bulkhead. Wales reached out to her, but she recovered herself and gave her shoulders a shake. 'I shall be all right, Jim. Go on deck now—do your best for my husband.'

He knew she meant the ship. He said, 'I'll do that, ma'am, I promise you.' He flushed a little and turned away, making back for the deck. While the preparations for the repair went ahead he paced the poop, his eyes lifted constantly to observe the direction and strength of any change in the wind. For now, all seemed set fair still; the sky was blue, with only faint twists of practically motionless cloud hanging suspended below its arc. The air was cold but brisk and there was no feeling of wind or rain to come; over the side the water, green in colour, was crystal clear. Wales could see the bottom: clean soft sand, leading up to the sunken treachery of the rock slope. Like gold that sand was, he thought. He listened to the sounds along the deck as planks were brought up from below, and canvas. Canvas brought poor Underwood to mind again: he would tell off the sailmaker to prepare a canvas shroud when the work on deck was completed. The body would have to be kept in the coolest possible place and that was likely to be the lifeboat once it had been hoisted again to its chocks and the tarpaulin cover rigged.

Wales turned his attention back to the possibilities of wind and within the next half-hour noticed the dark trail along the horizon to the south-west, a trail of black that held an ominous look when seen from the motionless deck of a stricken vessel. If that darkening meant a real blow from the south-west quarter, then they would all be in real trouble.

Wales moved to the fore rail of the poop. 'Bosun,' he called. 'One moment, if you please.'

O'Connor moved aft, enquiringly. 'What's the trouble, then?'

'Look to the sou'-west. D'you think that means wind?'

O'Connor looked, screwing up his eyes. Then he laughed. 'I'd doubt if it means wind, Mister Wales! Though there's some out there all right...blowing the smoke about!'

'Smoke?'

'Aye, smoke, for that's what it is—not a cloud. If I were you I'd get me below for the skipper's telescope and take a proper look.'

Wales went down the companion ladder in a bound, coming back with Landon's telescope. He ran with it along the deck and climbed the main shrouds to the crosstrees. Adjusting the glass he focused on the smoke. From his higher position he could now see the source of that smoke? it was billowing in clouds from the tall funnels of no fewer than six steamers, still hull-down and so far unidentifiable.

He called down to O'Connor. 'You're right, bosun. Six steamers out there.'

'Six, eh? Now, you'll know what that means, Mister Wales?'

'You tell me!'

'It won't be the PSNC out of Liverpool... when did you ever hear of six steamers together, carrying freight or passengers? They'll be the Queen's ships, Mister—men-o'-war.'

Wales blew out a long breath; this could be salvation. He remained in the crosstrees until he was able to identify the ships positively. He saw that the bosun had been right again. Six black-hulled ironclads with yellow- and white-painted upperworks and buff masts and funnels, with green boot-topping, their gunturrets trained smartly to the fore-and-aft line, were steaming majestically in formation from the south-west, apparently directing their course to pass the coastlines some ten miles out to seaward. At a guess that was a heavy cruiser squadron. Wales snapped the telescope shut and slid down fast to the deck. Running to the cabin he entered unceremoniously and reported to Landon.

'Warships, sir, about ten miles to the sou'-west. Shall I signal them, sir—ask for assistance, though I believe we can manage on our own—'

'Bluejackets,' Landon said somewhat mysteriously.

'Bluejackets, sir?'

'Yes. Men to help in the search for Chardonnet.' Landon sat up, shaky still, eyes over-bright but full of his old determination now. 'I'll come on deck, Wales...no, my dear,' he added as his wife began to remonstrate. 'I have my duty and I shall do it whatever happens.' He spoke again to Wales. 'Send up the distress rockets in the meantime and let me know at once when the warships answer. Take the International Code of Signals from the bookcase in the saloon. Quickly now!'

'Aye, aye, sir.' Wales turned around as Landon, still disregarding his wife's protests, put a leg out of the bunk. On deck again he passed the order to the bosun; within minutes a rocket had streaked from the *Pass of Drumochter*'s poop and was heading out across the sky to seaward to burst in a spray of stars. Two minutes later it was followed by another. Within seconds of a third rocket being fired, Wales, watching again through the telescope, saw a string of coloured bunting being hoisted from the flat deck of the leading ship in the line. He read off the signal with the help of O'Connor and the code book: *I am altering to your assistance.* As Landon reached the poop, they saw the men-o'-war altering course towards them.

Some ten cables'-lengths off the port beam of the *Pass of Drumochter*, the warships, having reduced speed, thrashed their screws astern on the signal from the flag and then lay hove-to, with enough distance between each to ensure safety. The ships—they turned out to be Her Majesty's armoured cruisers *Lord Cochrane, Defiance, Thunderer, Devastation, Powerful* and *Andromeda,* forming the 14th Cruiser Squadron—would undoubtedly have gladdened the eyes of Horatio Mainprice; but the men aboard the windjammer watched their arrival with much more mixed feelings. Always there had been intense rivalry between the Queen's service and the merchantmen, each to a greater or lesser degree denigrating the other when their paths happened to cross. There was still even now in the mid-nineties the taint of the press gang about the Royal Navy and, more often than not, a bloated pomposity and conceit about naval officers that made them ridiculous in the eyes of overworked masters and mates whose ships constantly kept the seas while men-o'-war lay snug and safe in harbour, giving leave to their ships' companies. Nevertheless, at this moment the Queen's men would be welcome enough; and even though O'Connor and Dabbs both spat over the side as they watched a cutter pulling away from the *Lord Cochrane's* starboard accommodation-ladder, they each had a feeling of satisfaction that, if the Old Man could talk fast enough, a few hundred armed bluejackets and marines might soon be scouring the Chilean hinterland for a smell of the Frenchy. It would be well worth a little civility to the brassbounders to achieve that; a fact that every man aboard seemed to hoist in without being told. So they watched with hope and interest as the cutter was pulled across the gap.

Seated in the sternsheets was an officer, and just forward of him a man armed with a cutlass who seemed to be a petty officer.

Landon ordered a rope ladder to be put over the side. The cutter came alongside this and the officer, getting to his feet, reached out for it. The hands grappled him over the bulwarks as he came up, followed by the petty officer and a seaman. The officer—someone aboard the flagship had used commonsense and tact, for he was wearing the two intertwined gold stripes of a lieutenant in the Royal Naval Reserve, indicating that he was by profession a merchant service officer—instantly recognized Landon as the Master.

Saluting, he said, 'My Captain's compliments, sir. He'd be glad to know what he can do to assist.'

'Thank you,' Landon said. He shook the Lieutenant's hand warmly. He then introduced Wales. The reserve officer nodded in a friendly way.

'My name's Blake,' he said. 'By way of introducing my ship...*Lord Cochrane's* the flagship of Rear-Admiral Pierce, commanding the South Atlantic Squadron. We've just rounded Cape Horn, to carry out goodwill visits to Chilean and Peruvian ports. A trifle off our usual station...but it's all in the day's work.' He smiled. 'Now, sir: I'm not unfamiliar with square rig—I served my time with Iredale and Carter, out of Liverpool—'

'The *Dales* ships—*Foyledale, Wensleydale*...I know them. Fine ships all.'

'Fine ships indeed, sir. We shall speak the same language. What do you want of us?'

Landon gestured for'ard. 'You can see for yourself how I'm placed. That, however, is not my main worry. I believe I can effect a repair with my own resources—though I'd be grateful if a ship of your squadron could stand by me in case of bad weather, and then perhaps tend me to sea when I'm able to float off.' He took a deep breath and steadied himself momentarily against the bulwarks. 'I'm anxious about a—deserter, a man who killed my Second Mate after putting my ship aground and then—then deserted. I have a landing party ashore at this moment, but its numbers are few. I request assistance urgently, Mr Blake.'

Lieutenant Blake's face was serious: this, he had not expected. 'You'll understand I cannot commit my Captain in advance. I must return aboard, and perhaps you'd care to accompany me, sir?'

Landon shook his head. 'I'm sorry—I must not leave my ship in danger. I'm sure your Captain will understand that. But I must ask you to hurry. The man is, as I have said, a murderer. Not once, but twice. He's wanted by the police in England for killing the First Mate of his last ship.' He added, with a catch in his voice, 'Now, you are wondering how he came to be aboard my ship...I shall explain everything when the time comes, but it is a long story and we may not have much time.'

While they waited for Blake to return from the *Lord Cochrane* the word went round the ship like a bush fire that the Frenchy was in fact twice a murderer and that Landon had known this all along. O'Connor asked the Captain the question direct, having been one of those who had overheard the conversation with Blake, and he got a direct answer.

'Yes, O'Connor. But there will be no details given for now.'

'There'll be trouble over this, sir.'

'Then it will be my trouble alone. No one else is involved.'

O'Connor said, his face grim, 'I was meaning trouble with the hands, sir. They're not going to like having been shipmates with a murderer. All unknowing, sir.'

Landon gave him a long, straight look. 'I give you my word, there were extenuating circumstances in the case of the first murder. I have heard Chardonnet's story. You have not.'

'No, sir, that's—'

'There is of course nothing to be said for Chardonnet in the case of Mr Underwood. But I cannot risk trouble now, O'Connor. Chardonnet will be brought to justice, you may be sure of that. In the meantime, I rely on you to keep the men in check. Mr Wales is able but inexperienced. I have no other officers now. Do your best, O'Connor.'

'Aye, sir, that I will.' O'Connor fingered the stubble on his cheeks and pursed his lips doubtfully as he went for'ard. There was going to be a good deal of tooth-sucking going on and it was unlikely to be too restrained. But maybe with armed bluejackets and marines in the offing, the hands might not be too eager to make real trouble.

Blake was back within the hour with satisfactory news. The Admiral had authorized a landing party of one hundred seamen armed with rifles and bayonets and a detachment of the Royal Marine Light Infantry, plus petty officers and leading hands, also a lieutenant of marines, a gunner and a couple of midshipmen with Blake himself in overall command. This party would be provided by *HMS Andromeda,* to which ship Blake would be transferred once the *Pass of Drumochter* had been floated off with her deserter recovered. Thereafter the cruiser would remain standing by the windjammer. In the meantime the Flag, with the remainder of the squadron, would steam away to carry on their duties to the north.

Already, as Blake had been on his way back from the *Lord Cochrane*, a number of boats had been lowered from the *Andromeda's* davits and filled to capacity with the seamen and marines of the landing parties. As each filled it was pulled away without delay towards the *Pass of Drumochter*, there to discharge and return for another load. While these movements were in progress the five other warships, smoke belching blackly from their tall funnels, steamed away with strings of bunting fluttering from their signal halliards, and were soon out of sight to the north. Once they had gone, the *Andromeda* also made smoke and, with her engines moving dead slow, crept a little closer inshore and let go a bower anchor and stern anchor, at the same time swinging her turrets so that the great gun-barrels were brought to bear over the coastline.

Jim Wales, watching, thought with a grin that young Horatio Mainprice really was missing something. The windjammer's decks were beginning to ring increasingly and strangely to the heavy stamp of RMLI boots, the crash of rifle butts and an odd assortment of unaccustomed orders from petty officers and sergeants and the hoarse, raucous pontificating of a tubby little warrant officer—Mr Robbins, Gunner RN. In his own ship, Jim Wales thought, Mr Robbins would be just about the equivalent of O'Connor; but here he seemed to be putting the fear of God into all the Queen's men from Lieutenant Blake downwards with his bounce and bluster.

Wales caught O'Connor's eye as Mr Robbins' voice echoed over the deck from for'ard to aft, and gave a broad wink. Horatio Mainprice, little blighter, was welcome to this sort of carry-on and good luck to him. As for Wales, he preferred the sea to the barrack square. Aided by O'Connor and the carpenter, he tackled the gunner on the subject of weight distribution. As he pointed out acidly, caring nothing for Mr Robbins' dignity, the navy was in a fair way to sinking the ship altogether if they didn't disperse aft.

That afternoon Landon sent his written

report across to the *Andromeda* and a formal enquiry was conducted into Underwood's murder. The warship's medical officer was sent across to examine the body and after this it was taken out in one of the cruiser's cutters, sewn into its canvas shroud by the *Pass of Drumochter's* sailmaker, and committed to deep water by the Chaplain from the warship.

In the meantime the landing parties had been put ashore by the boats, which had proceeded inwards through one of the fiord-like sea openings. There they had been split into three main groups, one to search north, another east and the third to the south though it was considered fairly unlikely the Frenchman would have made his way south to the colder and more desolate areas running down towards Punta Arenas. If the party heading south had not picked up any traces within forty-eight hours, they were under orders to turn back for the disembarkation point where fresh instructions would be sent from the cruiser.

Two mornings later Patience and his men, coming to the end of the forest, reached a clearing that seemed to extend for some considerable distance to east and west, with another section of forest ahead to the north.

There were no signs of life; and now it was raining heavily out of a grey, desolate sky. Patience halted the hands, who were close to dropping by this time. 'Another rest,' he said wearily. 'Back in the trees again, where it's dry.' He gestured towards the foliage above. 'With all the timber overhead, rain'd take a month to penetrate I shouldn't wonder.'

They turned and trailed back in again.

Tom Chatto felt he couldn't go a step further until he'd had a good long sleep. He flung himself on the ground, careless of insects or of anything else that might lurk in the forest undergrowth. His head reeled and his body was one vast ache; this was as bad in its way as battling against the westerlies off the Horn. But mind and body were too restless to allow him to sleep and he simply lay in a numbed stupor until Patience called to the men to come and get their ration of water and hard tack.

Tom pulled himself to his feet and collected two of the dry, weevilly biscuits and munched them. Then he lay down again, only to be called back on his feet by the Mate.

'Yes, sir?' he said.

'Here, boy. And you, Mainprice.' Patience, Tom found, had started pushing through the trees to the fringe once again. Tom followed as quickly as he could and joined Patience by the edge of the clearing. The Mate took his arm. Behind them Horatio limped up, his face full of unspilled complaint as Patience, hearing his approach, glanced round.

'Holy Jesus,' Patience said in feigned astonishment. 'What's this, then? In dire straits, are you, without nanny to kiss you better?'

Horatio flushed. 'I'm dead tired, that's—'

'Sir.'

'Sir. Also, I don't think we're doing any good. We're just wasting our time.'

'Well, well! I see. So what in God's name, Admiral bloody Mainprice, does your honour suggest we should do instead —eh?'

'I don't know,' the apprentice answered surlily. 'From all I've seen since I joined that ship, it's not my job to think.'

'And you're quite right, Admiral Mainprice, quite right—'

'Oh, for God's sake!' Horatio had seen red; his voice rose to a screech. 'Stop calling me Admiral Mainprice, can't you!'

Patience started in sheer surprise. Then he gave a cold smile and said with exaggerated politeness, 'Don't you like it, then?'

'No!' Horatio glared back.

'I see. Well, well. Just move around me, boy, and take a look at the clearing, will you. I'm sure you will...seeing as I'm asking nicely. Eh?'

Horatio's mouth set obstinately and he appeared about to refuse. Patience's heavy face darkened. *'Move, damn you!'* he grated. Horatio moved. When he was in a suitable position, the Mate took a step backwards then swung his leg viciously. The leather seaboot took Horatio full on the backside, with all Patience's weight behind it. Giving a shrill cry of pain and shock, the apprentice staggered forward in an undignified lurch, out into the clearing, where he tripped and fell flat on his face.

'Don't come back,' Patience called after him, 'till you've done what I was about to tell you to do—which is, spy out the land to the west'ard. See if you can find anything that looks like a trail. If you do, come back pronto and report.'

Patience swung round on Tom, who was grinning at the helpless fury in Horatio's face as he scrambled to his feet. 'You can wipe that smirk off your ugly mug, Chatto. You're going to do the same as *Admiral* Mainprice, only you'll take the east'ard tack, all right?'

'Aye, aye, sir.' Tom hesitated. 'What sort of things shall I look out for, sir?'

'Same as Mainprice. Tracks, boy, tracks! *Leads.'* Patience spread his hands wide. '*I* can't tell you more than that. I've been away from the land longer than you have. Use your brain. Anything that looks unusual or out of place—back you come and report.'

Tom went out into the clearing.

He looked towards the west, where Horatio Mainprice was mooching along sullenly, hurt dignity and anger in his every movement, then he turned and headed up towards the east where the ground began climbing to the foothills and more virgin forest. His feet squelched into soggy ground as he went along; the teeming rain soaked into his clothing, coldly. It was a miserable and depressing scene; but the

West of Ireland had accustomed him to living with almost incessant rain and he was able to take it, though he longed for one of the deanery's blazing turf fires to dry him out afterwards—that, and a good square meal, and the servants to attend to his wants. But he couldn't help smiling as he trudged along, looking out for something to report to the Mate: what would his family think if they could see him now, out in the backwoods of Chile, beyond the fringe of civilization, chasing after a murderer...it wasn't what his father would ever imagine he had allowed his son to go to sea for. Brother Edward in his country parsonage would no doubt be scandalized. Such thoughts led Tom on to other contemplations: if ever he got back to Moyna after all this, how would his family and their mundane lives and surroundings appear to him?

Already he felt his whole outlook to be changed by his experiences aboard a deep-water sailing ship, by his close personal contact with people very different from any he had known before—save only Uncle Benjamin—and by the very real dangers he had shared with those people.

Real dangers, real people. In a word—men. Cruel, some of them, spiteful as Patience could so often be, coarse, many of them loose-living drunkards when ashore, but men all of them. How, then, would the deanery appear, and the excellent diocesan ladies—the bishop's wife, the canons' wives and daughters, the womenfolk of the lesser parochial clergy?

Tom sighed; he was fond of his home and often enough yearned to see it all again, but he could foresee a certain element of boredom to come when he would have to sit of an evening and listen to tales of sewing parties and good works and church outings, and the occasional exciting flurry of tennis on the deanery lawn, or croquet, or a jumble sale in the bishop's grounds...

Tom was in a reverie and after a while he realized guiltily that he'd been paying little attention to what he was supposed to be doing. The going was extremely heavy and he was still not far from Patience and the others. He pushed his personal thoughts into the back of his mind and concentrated on the job in hand, and it was only a matter of minutes after this that his eye caught a movement in the trees, some way ahead to his right.

Stopping dead, he crouched low.

Watching closely, he saw the movement again.

He saw it was a man. A man weaving around in the trees almost drunkenly.

A very tired man, an exhausted man?

*Chardonnet?*

It had to be the Frenchman. Cautiously, Tom wriggled his body round and moved on his stomach, back to where he had left Patience. Filthy, flesh torn by the undergrowth and the rough ground, he reached the rest of the party and stood up in the cover of the trees.

'Well, boy?'

'I think I've found him, sir! Chardonnet.'

'*Have* you, by God? Where?' There was a sadistic gleam in the Mate's eye but Tom was too full of his discovery to notice Patience's expression.

He said, 'Back the way I came from, sir. I can lead you right to him. I don't think he'll have moved far. He looked pretty well done in, sir.

Patience nodded. 'We'll move in on him at once.' He called the fo'c'sle hands to their feet and they moved out, with

Tom ahead of the party and Patience right behind him. They didn't trouble to conceal themselves and they moved fast. When they had reached roughly the area where Tom had seen the movement, a man stepped out from the trees. It was Chardonnet. He was haggard, his clothing was torn and his flesh was ripped by brambles and the flailing of branches, but he had pulled himself together and was walking out from cover with some trace still of the swagger that Tom had always associated with him, and he was smiling derisively as if capture was of no consequence to him at all.

'It is an inhospitable and terrible country, this,' he called out. 'Me, I have had enough! I surrender.'

'The devil you do,' Patience said with a harsh laugh. He pushed past Tom, thrusting the apprentice heavily aside. Before anyone could react, he had lifted Landon's pistol and fired. His aim was true. Chardonnet stopped very suddenly in his somewhat pathetic swagger, looked immensely surprised, jerked two or three times and then fell flat.

# CHAPTER 14

By next morning the cruiser's Captain, having read Landon's summary and having seen certain signals from Lieutenant Blake, had intimated that he wished a personal report from the *Pass of Drumochter*'s Master. So Landon had been obliged after all to repair aboard when the Captain's galley was sent across to bring him off.

Landon was weak and shaky still, and his head and shoulders were heavily bandaged. Stepping onto the *Andromeda*'s quarterdeck from the accommodation ladder, which was attended by four seamen and a corporal of the Royal Marine Light Infantry, together with the sword-belted Officer of the Watch, Landon was escorted to the Captain's quarters, proceeding along a white-painted steel alley-way lined with racked rifles under the charge of a sentry; and into a well-furnished cabin where Captain Harrington rose from before a roll-top bureau to welcome him.

'Good of you to come across, Captain,'

he said. They shook hands. 'Please be seated.' He indicated an easy chair and Landon sat, placing his tall hat on the deck of the cabin and folding his arms across his chest. Harrington, a hawk-faced man with mutton-chop whiskers and a coldly patrician manner, raked his visitor with a hard stare that left Landon with a naked feeling. 'Will you take a drink?'

Landon shook his head. 'Thank you, Captain, no.'

'As you please,' Harrington said indifferently. A steward was standing by, deferentially, in a starched white tunic with shining brass buttons. Harrington nodded at this man, who turned towards a mahogany cabinet and then approached his Captain with a crystal tumbler of whisky on a silver salver. Without a word Harrington took the tumbler, sat again at his desk, sipped the whisky and nodded again at the steward, who silently left the cabin.

Harrington stared at Landon. 'Well?' he said.

'First,' Landon answered, after clearing his throat heavily, for he was unaccustomedly nervous of his future now, 'I wish to thank you most gratefully for all the assistance you and your officers and men are giving my ship. This—'

'Yes, yes.' Harrington drummed his fingers on his bureau. He glanced upwards in irritation as a tramp of feet sounded through the deckhead, then turned back to Landon. 'What concerns me more at the moment, Captain, is the man you brought from Liverpool—the murderer Fontanet.'

'Of course,' Landon said. 'He was found stowed away, as no doubt you'll have read in my report—'

'Yes. The fact remains, does it not, that you failed to hand him over to the authorities in Recife—even though before you left the port you were aware he was a common murderer. You do not question this?'

'No,' Landon answered quietly, meeting the naval Captain's hard stare without a flicker. 'It is true enough.'

'Then why?'

'You have my report, Captain. There were the two reasons. I was short-handed and was facing a passage of Cape Horn. And the man had risked his life to save that of—'

'Yes.' Harrington paused. 'What did you intend doing with him ultimately?'

'At the time he put my ship aground...I had not finally decided. I would most probably have carried him on to Sydney.'

'Oh? Why not land him at Valparaiso?'

Landon shrugged. 'I am sure, sir, you know these dago ports as well as I.'

There was a glimmer of a smile on Harrington's face as he said, 'H'm...I take your point. But the fellow was a damned Frenchman, not an Englishman.'

'He lived and breathed nevertheless,' Landon said shortly.

There was an irritable laugh. 'That was not what I meant and you know it. What was to be gained by taking a French national to a British colonial port such as Sydney?'

'Why, a greater chance of justice.'

'For a murderer?' Harrington's eyebrows went up sharply. 'A hangman's knot is justice for murder, wherever it's tied.'

'But you forget one thing, Captain.' Landon leaned forward and spoke earnestly. 'Until Fontanet left my ship—until he killed my Second Mate—he had been proven guilty of nothing. There had been no trial, he was not an escaped criminal in the proven sense of that word. His alleged crime had been committed in a British port. I considered he must have the fairest chance possible. Naturally, after the killing aboard my ship, it was very different.'

'You'd not have helped him thereafter?'

'No, certainly I would not.'

'You'd have landed him at Valparaiso?'

'Yes.'

'That would have been wise. I am glad to hear you say that—and I accept that you would indeed have done so.'

'Thank you,' Landon said stiffly.

Harrington got to his feet with an abrupt movement. 'Captain, I think at this stage there is little more that can usefully be said. Much will depend, as you'll of course realize, on the success or otherwise of the pursuit.'

'Of course.' Landon wiped sweat from his face. For a few moments he sat on, frowning and perturbed, seemingly irresolute, then reacted to Harrington's obvious impatience and rose to his feet. With a heavy heart he preceded the cruiser's Captain up on deck to be shown to the gangway to embark aboard the galley for the pull back to his ship.

They were coming back to the beach now,

heading by compass bearing through the forest.

They had Chardonnet's body with them, two men at a time taking turns at carrying it. They were a silent party mostly; they were too dog-tired for talk, and too pre-occupied. Patience had gone almost to pieces and had spent a good deal of the time muttering away to himself like a lunatic. After the shot had been fired one of the fo'c'sle hands had struck him down from behind. The Frenchy had been a murderer sure enough, but you didn't kill a man who'd already surrendered.

'Damn you to hell,' Patience had raved, picking himself up and looking white. 'I never heard him say anything about surrendering.'

That hadn't washed: they had all heard him shout out, 'The devil you do.'

'What if I did?' Patience had demanded, looking at the accusing faces all around him. 'What if I did? He'd have swung anyway.' After that Patience twisted himself into a knot trying to explain away his action. He hadn't meant to kill the Frenchy, only to scare him, to make sure he really did surrender without giving any further trouble. Words poured from him like vomit. It had been the only way to deal with a murderer, the only safe way for them all. He'd been acting for their safety, for their lives.

It was Tom who put it into words: Patience was himself a murderer now.

Waving their arms and shouting, the pursuit party attracted the attention of the hands working aboard the *Pass of Drumochter* and after some delay a boat was pulled inshore. Patience sat silent now in the sternsheets. He was a very frightened man.

There were cheers from along the deck as they approached, but these died away in an awed hush, a puzzled hush, as the body was seen. From the poop, his face still and drawn, Landon watched as it was hoisted aboard. As the Mate came over the side he called, 'Mr Patience, come aft, if you please.'

Slowly, Patience obeyed. 'Well, Mr Patience? I see Chardonnet is dead.'

'The man had to be shot.'

'Had to be, Mr Patience? He was armed, then?'

The answer came not from Patience but from a man below the break of

301

the poop. 'The Frenchy wasn't armed, Captain.' Patience turned and saw the crew assembled in the waist, staring aft, every man watching himself and the Master. 'Captain,' he said uncertainly, 'this looks like trouble.'

'An understatement, Mr Patience! You must tell me the truth—for all our sakes.'

Patience licked at his lips. 'I shot him. I had to. He was a murderer, wasn't he? He'd deliberately put the ship aground. I know that's not absolutely proved, but he must have done, it stands to reason, doesn't it?'

Landon made no comment. He asked, 'Were you...angry when you shot him?'

'Well, who wouldn't be?' Patience looked the Captain straight in the eye, brazening it out now. 'I repeat, he was a killer—and a damn shipbreaker—and he'd been a deserter, hadn't he, before any of this? He was due to swing anyway and we all know it. The way he died...wasn't it easier than a rope?'

Landon turned away and paced the poop, backwards and forwards, his hands clasped behind his back. He heard the murmurs from the men on deck, felt the concentration of everyone on what his next words might be. Turning forward he went to the rail and stared down. He said, 'Back to your work all of you. There's much to be done.'

'What are you going to do about Patience, Captain?' a voice called.

'What is between Mr Patience and myself is my concern,' Landon answered. He looked farther for'ard where the naval party had also stopped work and were watching, then looked back at his own crew. 'Go back to your duties immediately or there'll be trouble. Bosun?'

O'Connor turned and faced the fo'c'sle hands. 'Captain's right. It'll be sorted out, never fear, and for my part I reckon Mr Patience did right. Why should we bother our heads over the bloody Frenchy when all's said and done?'

There were several shouts of assent to this; Patience looked happier. But there were shouts against O'Connor's words as well and he had barely finished speaking when the fighting started. There was a strong body of opinion against the First Mate, men who had had it in for him for a long while past and who now saw their chance of getting back at him. Tom was sent flying against the main fiferail and scrambled up, intending to get clear away from the brawling fo'c'sle hands.

He heard Landon's shout: *'Mr Blake!'*

The RNR lieutenant waited no longer. He ordered his men in, an overwhelming force against the ship's crew. That night there were any number of sore heads and bloodied noses but there was outward peace.

Just before sundown Landon waited again upon the cruiser's Captain, to whom he made his further report.

Harrington listened closely and with a serious face and when Landon had finished he said, 'From your point of view it seems the best possible ending, Captain—in all the circumstances. I shall need to give more thought to the position of your First Mate, and to your possible crew troubles.' He sat back in his swivel chair, finger-tips touching in a parsonic manner, eyes shrewdly thoughtful. 'Now—have you anything further you wish to say, Captain Landon?'

Landon shook his head. 'No. Nothing further. You have the facts. Now I must abide by your advice as to the future.'

'Advice, yes. No more than that. The

decisions will not be mine to make, of course, but I can offer recommendations in the proper quarter and I believe I shall be listened to.' Harrington paused. 'Captain...you have never mentioned to me that the man told you his name was Chardonnet, whereas in fact, as we now know—since he admitted it to you—that it was Fontanet.'

Landon said, 'It is in my earlier report.'

'Yes. I'm aware of that. I meant, you've not spoken of it to me, either when you last came aboard, or now. And in your report, which I have here in my bureau, you appear to note it merely in passing as it were. Why is this?'

Landon showed his surprise. 'It seemed of little importance in the circumstances.'

'Oh? But surely...could it not have caused you some confusion, Captain— some doubt in your mind, when the British consul at Recife told you about a murderer named *Fontanet*—doubt that your stowaway was in fact that same man?'

'None at all,' Landon answered shortly. 'It was perfectly obvious to me, as I think it would have been to you.'

'H'm.' Harrington cleared his throat, fiddled with a pencil from his bureau.

'But—do you not see—as an excuse...?'

'I am not in the habit of making excuses, Captain Harrington. I make none now. I take full responsibility for my actions be they right or be they wrong.'

His tone had been angry but Harrington appeared not to take any offence. 'I see. Admirable principles...I think you are a man after my own heart. Had you answered differently, I believe I would have been much disappointed. However...' He said nothing further but rose to his feet and paced the day cabin with short, brisk steps, four one way, four the other, brushing continually past Landon's knees, his hands with the four gold rings of his rank on the cuffs of his uniform jacket held behind his back. For a full five minutes he paced, then suddenly he stopped in front of his visitor and looked down upon him.

He said, 'I have an estate in Norfolk— Brinsthorpe. I have an idea that if, say, a gipsy or a poacher were to save my wife from drowning in a pond in my park, and I were subsequently to be approached by the police about some misdemeanour on that man's part...I have an idea I might well offer the police no help. I might offer the miscreant sanctuary from the law if it should happen I were short of gamekeepers at the time!' He was smiling broadly now. 'You shouldn't take me too literally, Captain—but, you see, I think we are perhaps birds of a feather. And in any event I believe you to be undoubtedly a man of honour.'

Landon inclined his head. 'Thank you.'

'You have given every assistance in the pursuit of the man and he was in fact caught. Yes, I shall make my recommendations to our consul in Valparaiso and to the authorities at home. I think you have little reason to worry.'

'Captain—as I have told you—the man is dead.'

'Through no fault of your own. The position of your First Mate is of course different. I feel that in his own interest he should be transferred aboard my ship as far as Valparaiso—and then we shall see. You agree?'

Heavily, Landon nodded. 'It would be better, yes. I shall feel the loss, however. He's a first-rate seaman.'

'You have others. If necessary I can assist with hands.'

'Thank you,' Landon said, 'but I'll sail my own ship with my own men. I shall manage—we'll be in easier waters once we're away again.'

'That's so, and this we must now discuss,' Harrington said briskly, and went on to deal with the various questions of sea-worthiness that would arise following the grounding; and half an hour later accompanied Landon to the head of the accommodation ladder, having sent orders ahead to the gangway for the galley to be called away once again.

As Landon went over the cruiser's side, Harrington stood at the salute. While the galley was pulled away he spoke to the lieutenant on watch. 'A fine breed of men, Mr Spencer-Lyte, and a harder life for them than any of *us* have known.' He stood for a while looking out across the dark water as the galley pulled into the night, dwindling to a pin-point of her stern-light, then turned away abruptly and strode off the quarterdeck.

Back aboard Landon's ship the repair work continued through the night, the shipwrights loaned by the cruiser assisting the carpenter and crew. Within another forty-eight hours the outboard repairs had been completed, the men having worked over the side during the spells of low water when the whole of the damaged stem had been left high and dry. The water was then pumped out of her and after that, and after Landon's close inspection with Dabbs and the chief shipwright from the *Andromeda,* the business of refloating was put in hand.

In the absence of Patience, signed off articles and transferred with his baggage and with Chardonnet's corpse to the warship—the corpse would be kept in the *Andromeda*'s cold storage—it was Jim Wales who supervised the removal of much of the cargo from the fore hold and its temporary transferral aft so as to lighten the fore part of the ship. Once she was off the rocks and the makeshift repair finally rounded-off inboard, this cargo was re-stowed and, within four hours thereafter, the *Pass of Drumochter* was as ready as possible for sea.

When this was reported to the *Andromeda,* orders were signalled across the water that the naval party was to return; and at once Lieutenant Blake mustered his men. As the cruiser's boats came in the bluejackets and marines from the landing parties, who had returned empty-handed from the shore earlier, piled aboard and were pulled back to their ship. When they had all gone, word was passed along the windjammer's deck that the Master was to speak to all hands, who were to muster below the break of the poop.

Landon gave them all the facts.

He added, 'The ship will sail immediately for Valparaiso and *HMS Andromeda* will stand by us all the way in case of any difficulty. All repair work will be examined at Valparaiso and made good where necessary whilst we are discharging cargo. We shall sail for Sydney Heads as soon as possible. In the absence of Mr Patience, Mr Wales continues temporarily as First Mate.'

He turned to Jim Wales, who was standing beside him. 'Report when ready, if you please, Mr Wales. I shall be in the saloon.'

'Aye, aye, sir.' Wales went down the ladder to the deck below. 'Bosun, have the lifeboat standing by to turn us for the open sea. Once we're round and with way on us, I'll want all canvas shaken out to the t'gallants'ls and all available hands ready at the braces. All right?'

O'Connor grinned and spat into his

palms. 'All right it is, sir!' He ran for'ard to the fo'c'sle head and began shouting the hands to their stations.

Wales put an arm around Tom's shoulder. 'I'm bound to use Ted Allan as a sort of acting Second Mate,' he said, 'but I'm leaving you to take charge in the waist and see to it that the yards are properly braced whenever I give the order. You'll need to be smart, and you'll need to chase the fo'c'sle crowd. They'll hate taking it from you, but it'll be necessary and it'll be first-rate experience. You'll be all right, Tom.'

A puff of wind, a mere capful, met them once they were round and headed seaward. The sails, which had been sent aloft to their yards after the bow had been freed, were shaken out along the jackstays. The lifeboat was hoisted and secured for sea on the skids. As the yards were braced round to catch the light wind to the best advantage, the *Pass of Drumochter* moved slowly, very slowly out into the Pacific and, when she was well clear of the land, was brought onto her northerly course for Valparaiso.

She passed close across the bow of

the cruiser, whose decks were lined with seamen dressed in white duck suits and sennit hats that came off to be waved vigorously as cheers rang out across the water. There was a heartening quality in those cheers and Tom, glancing briefly aft as he stood by the weather braces in the waist, saw Landon on the poop with Mary at his side, standing stiff and straight like a rock. He saw the Old Man lift his tall hat in acknowledgement of Captain Harrington's salute from his navigating bridge; and then more wind met them as they came out from the lee of the land and Tom became busy as the sails filled and drew the *Pass of Drumochter* on more swiftly, to leave the cruiser astern in her streaming wake. But already the warship was belching plumes of thick, black smoke from her funnels and soon after this Tom saw from the kerfuffle under her stern that she was making way through the water.

She was a majestic sight. Horatio Mainprice seemed quite overcome...

This Large Print Book for the Partially sighted, who cannot read normal print, is published under the auspices of

## THE ULVERSCROFT FOUNDATION

# Other MAGNA Mystery Titles In Large Print

**WILLIAM HAGGARD**
The Vendettists

**C. F. ROE**
Death By Fire

**MARJORIE ECCLES**
Cast A Cold Eye

**KEITH MILES**
Bullet Hole

**PAULINE G. WINSLOW**
A Cry In The City

**DEAN KOONTZ**
Watchers

**KEN McCLURE**
Pestilence

## Other MAGNA Mystery Titles
## In Large Print